T0118544

Meditation
The Ultimate In Healing

"Do not treat the disease, instead treat the patient,"
Medicine considers each disease in man separately. This is
the approach that analyzes disease as a part.

Taoshobuddha

FOREWORD
DR. C.H. RAMNARINE, MBBS

authorHOUSE®

AuthorHouse™
1663 Liberty Drive
Bloomington, IN 47403
www.authorhouse.com
Phone: 1-800-839-8640

© 2012 by Taoshobuddha. All rights reserved.

No part of this book may be reproduced, stored in a retrieval system, or transmitted by any means without the written permission of the author.

Cover design and graphics: Swami Anand Neelamber

Published by AuthorHouse   07/02/2012

ISBN: 978-1-4772-1424-4 (sc)
ISBN: 978-1-4772-1423-7 (e)

Any people depicted in stock imagery provided by Thinkstock are models, and such images are being used for illustrative purposes only.
Certain stock imagery © Thinkstock.

This book is printed on acid-free paper.

Because of the dynamic nature of the Internet, any web addresses or links contained in this book may have changed since publication and may no longer be valid. The views expressed in this work are solely those of the author and do not necessarily reflect the views of the publisher, and the publisher hereby disclaims any responsibility for them.

First, love gives you unity in your innermost core.
Then you are no more a body. No more a mind,
no more a soul.

You are simply one. Unnamed, undefined,
unclassified! No more determinate, definable,
no more comprehensible.

A mystery, a joy, a surprise, jubilation, and
a great celebration!
A BEING ALONE!

When you sit silently watching your breath, you are connected to the unconscious layers through the mind. You are connected to suppressed emotions both at the personal and social level. Also, you are connected to the muscle and the physical system of karma. Then you can clear out every knot, thus clearing the body of all karmas.

No particular technique is complete to clear it. However, the Rolfing or Alexander technique, or Patterning and sensory awareness can clear the body of such tensions. But, when we stop a technique for a certain time, the body does not remain clear. This requires a constant attention to our bodies and our physical systems. Breathing is the most important of these. This is why these meditations.

TAOSHOBUDDHA—*MEDITATION THE WAY TO SELF REALIZATION*:
STERLING PUBLISHERS PVT LTD., NEW DELHI
INDIA 2008

The word '**Taoshobuddha**' comes from three words, 'tao,' 'sho,' and 'Buddha'. The word Tao was coined by the Chinese master, Lau Tzu. It means that which is and cannot be put into words. It is unknown and unknowable. It can only be experienced and not expressed in words. Its magnanimity cannot be condensed into finiteness. The word Sho implies, that which is vast like the sky and deep like an ocean and carries within its womb a treasure. It also means one on whom the existence showers its blessings. And lastly the word Buddha implies the Enlightened One; one who has arrived home.

Thus, TAOSHOBUDDHA implies one who is existential, on whom the existence showers its blessings and one who has arrived home. THE ENLIGHTENED ONE!

CONTENTS

SECTION 1
BODY MEDITATIONS

SECTION 2
MIND MEDITATIONS

SECTION 3
THE BODY—MIND BALANCING!

SECTION 4
MEDITATION THE ULTIMATE IN HEALING!

PREFACE

Mind wonders from where the healing can really begin. Physical body is mere showcase definitely it cannot be the beginning. Can you start at bio-plasmic level? Or you still have to go a step beyond. There are so many unresolved issues in each one of you that need to be addressed before the healing can really begin. All these issues are stored in the fathomless zero that occupied the world. The journey of healing has to begin from this point.

Meditation, on the other hand, considers man himself as a disease that comes to man because of inner imbalance between consciousness, ego, and mind and then disappears. Therefore Meditation is the Ultimate in Healing.

Ever since **'Meditation the way to Self Realization'** came into the market in 2008 the need is felt for **'Meditations to Balance Body and Mind'**. Also I had spoken that certain chapters and topics will need further elaboration. This present work is the outcome of such an understanding. This is the continuation of the first chapter **'What is meditation?'** and the last **'Meditation and HEALING'** in the book **'Meditation the Way to Self Realization'**. The book ended with MEDITATION AND HEALING as the last chapter. This present work is the continuation from where **'Meditation the way to Self Realization'** had ended. So also is the process of transformation a continuum. For this the seeker goes through various stages as each stage leads into another.

It was the hour before Gods awake
Across the path of the divine events
The huge foreboding mind of night, alone
In her unlit temple of eternity,
Lay stretched immobile upon Silence's marge
Almost one felt, opaque, impenetrable
In the somber symbols of her eyeless muse
The abysm of the unbodied infinite;
A fathomless zero occupied the world.

[SRI AUROBINDO: SAVITRI BOOK 1 THE BOOK OF BEGINNING—
CANTO 1 THE SYMBOL DAWN]

This is an investigation how healing can happen. I begin this investigation with a passage from Sri Aurobindo's Savitri. The **fathomless** zero occupied the cosmos and your world of finiteness. It is out of this fathomless zero first evolved ether or sky. Then came air. Followed by fire, the remaining elements the water and the earth and thus life evolved! The Soul! The Mind! And the Physical Body! Your Physical Body is mere showcase of all that happens at other planes or bodies.

Then the question comes from where the healing can really begin. Since physical body is mere showcase definitely it cannot be the beginning. Can you start at bio-plasmic level? Or you still have to go a step beyond. There are so many unresolved issues in each one of you that need to be addressed before the healing can really begin. All these issues are stored in the fathomless zero that occupied the world. The journey of healing has to begin from this point.

Through these meditations I am creating inner balance between body and the mind. Only then you can attain to meditativeness. This process will continue until new man, one who is beyond body, mind, and intellect, is born out of you. I maybe or may not be here but this process of transformation will continue erelong. This is my promise to you. This is just the beginning.

You are, from the very beginning, a Buddha. To the very core of your being you are a Buddha. It is your nature. It is like water and ice: apart from water, no ice. Outside living beings, no Buddhas! Not knowing it is near, they seek it afar. What a pity! It is like one in the water who cries out for thirst! Also it is like the child of a rich house who has strayed away among the poor. The cause of your circling through the six worlds is that you are on the dark paths of ignorance. Dark path upon dark path treading! When shall you escape from cycle of birth-and-death?

The Zen meditation of the Mahayana is beyond all our praise. Giving and morality and the other perfections, taking of the name, repentance, discipline, and the many other right actions, all come back to the practice of meditation. By the merit of a single sitting he destroys innumerable accumulated sins. How should there be wrong paths for him?

Beloved friends I love you. Love is my message. Love is my being. Love is the communion. Love is oneness. Love is harmony both within and without. Love is bliss. Let it be your message too. Love is my color and my climate as well. To me, love is the only religion. All else is just unnecessary and therefore can be discarded. All else is nothing but dreams. A mental game! Love is the only substantial thing in life! All else is illusion. Let love grow in you and then god will be growing on its own accord. If you miss love you will miss god and all. Then life will be misery and despair.

There is no way to god without love. There is nothing more sublime than love. God can be forgotten but not love. If love is remembered, god will happen as a consequence. It happens as a consequence. God is the fragrance of love and nothing else. In fact there is no god but only godliness. There is no person like god anywhere. Drop all childish attitudes. Never go on searching for a father. Divineness is god is not.

When I say divineness is, I mean whatsoever is, is full of god. The entire creation is full of godliness. Only you need eyes to see this. The green of the trees! And the red of the flowers and the golden glow of the rising sun all are divine. A crow crying and a bird on the wing, a child giggling, and a dog barking all is divine. Nothing else exists.

The moment you ask 'where is god?' you have raised a wrong question. Because god cannot be indicated anywhere! He is not in any particular direction. He is not a particular thing either. He is not a particular being. God is universality. God is totality. God is hidden in the entire creation. Ask where god is not? Only then you have asked the right question. One of the Hindu scriptures *Isa Upanishad* begins with a beautiful sutra. To say that it is Hindu scripture is erroneous. Truth is not Hindu or Muslim. Truth is beyond all finiteness. The scripture begins:

'The entire cosmos is permeated by ever expanding consciousness or Isa referring to God. It is your realization now. And once you have realized this you can enjoy the fruits of the entire cosmos. Then the entire cosmos belongs to you and you belong to the whole.'

Such is the essence of spiritual life. Therefore for that right question and understanding you will have to prepare the soil of your awareness. If you are not in love, then what to say about god! Even you are not. I was thinking what should I give to you today? Because this is the dawn of a new awakening! I can share with you my love, my awareness, and my understanding now and ever.

This day Absolute consciousness incarnated as Krishna. This is the day when absolute consciousness saw for the first time the green of the trees and the blue of the skies. This was the day for the first time when Krishna opened his eyes and saw god all around. Of course the word 'god' did not exist at that moment. However all that he saw was god.

That is what I mean by love—A union. Because in a union those who join together remain separate from the rest. In a unity they dissolve. They melt into one another. They become one. And that moment I call the moment of truth. When love has given you unity! And oneness too!

First, love gives you unity in your innermost core. Then you are no more a body, no more a mind, no more a soul. You are simply one. Unnamed, undefined, unclassified! No more determinate, definable, no more comprehensible. A mystery, a joy, a surprise, jubilation, and a great celebration!

First, love gives you an inner unity. This is *fana* as Sufis call this happening. And when the inner unity has happened the second happens on its own! You are not to do anything for it. Then you start falling in unity with the whole beyond you. Then the drop disappears in the ocean and the ocean disappears into the drop. That moment, that moment of orgasm between you and the whole, is where you become a Buddha. That moment is the moment Buddha hood is imparted to you. This is ENLIGHTENMENT.

Love is the way of preparing the soil of your heart. If you are full of love, the world is full of God. They go parallel. They are part of one symphony. God is the echo from the universe. When you are in love, the echo is there. When you are not in love, how can there be an echo?

God is an echo that lingers in your heart like the dissolving notes of a melody that you have once heard in the wilderness. It is only you who are reflected again and again in millions of ways. It is you who are thrown back to yourself again and again. If you are in love, God is.

I was thinking what should I give to you today as my gift for the birthday of a Buddha? Then I remembered a saying of Buddha: 'the gift of truth excels all other gifts.' And my truth is love. Truth is solitary. Truth is love. AND THAT IS ALL YOU NEED TO DISCOVER DEEP WITHIN.

The word 'Truth' looks to me a little too dry and desert—like. I am not in much tune with the word 'Truth'. It looks too logical. It looks too prosaic. It gives you the feeling of philosophy, not of religion. It gives you the idea as if you have concluded. You have come to a conclusion. And there has been a syllogism behind it, argumentation and logic and reasoning.

Instead of 'Truth' 'LOVE' is my word. Love is of the heart. Truth is partial. Only your head is involved in Truth. In love you are involved as a totality. Your body, your mind, your soul, all is involved. Love makes you a unity. But not a union! Remember love is UNITY. My word is love.

So I say: My beloved ones, I love you. And I would like you to fill the whole world with love. Let that be your religion. Love is simply love. In love you can be a Christ. In love you can be a Buddha. But there is no Buddhist love and there is no Christian love. In love you disappear, your mind disappears. In love you come to an utter relaxation.

Something more about the strategy of the book! You are a structure of body-mind. Naturally, physiology looks into your body and its functioning and psychology looks into your mind and its functioning as well. And beyond this western psychology cannot go.

I call you a Buddha. Yes indeed you are that. And I speak to you of Buddhas. Because they have come to know a different space within themselves! A space which cannot be confined by the mind and which cannot be defined as part of the functioning of the mind!

That silent space when thoughts are no more! No ripples arise! This is the beginning of the psychology of the Buddhas. This is the realm to which master belong. To this realm I want to take you to. This is just the beginning.

This is my message as my gift to you. The celebration of 'Enlightenment' as the 'Ultimate Flowering of Your Being' NOW AND EVER AND ANON!

The book contains 27 different meditations as the Ultimate in Healing. Continue each meditation for a period of 7 days each. And then repeat to sustain the inner state of awareness. Life will undergo the process of transformation.

Allow the journey to continue. Then one day suddenly something happens. At this stage all efforts cease and you reach to the realm of effortlessness.

The journey from effort to effortlessness is the only journey. Thereafter is the life of serenity, blessing and blessedness. This is the realm of the being.

As part of strategy this book comes along with an Audio CD containing these twenty seven meditations in the voice of **TAOSHOBUDDHA**. The voice that creates the aura of meditativeness around you! Listen to these meditations in a sequence for a period of seven days each. As the process of meditation begins one day certainly you will attain to fruition.

In the preparation and presentation of this work many have helped in numerous ways. I am thankful to our Chief Editor, **MEDITATION TIMES**_{TM} and sound engineer Swami Anand Neelamber needs a special mention as without his soulful efforts works of such a magnitude are difficult to undertake. He is responsible for all editing, sound and recording of these audio and videos.

Thousands of listeners and supporters world over who listened to scores of meditations on **YOUTUBE.COM** and **TOTAL BHAKTI. COM** and forwarded their comments and suggestions. These Scores of meditations are being listened to in over one hundred countries in all the five continents. These always remain as beacon light and guiding force.

I am lovingly thankful to my friend and physician Dr. C.H. Ramnarine for his foreword. This bears testimony to the efforts put forward in creating a work of this nature. **I have known Dr. Ramnarine for over twenty years therefore his foreword and introduction is a befitting introduction to the work.**

It will be improper not to mention of the unconditional support of my wife Gita, daughter Dr. Sargam and son Vivek Mohan. They have helped in their own unique way.

Last but not least, Professor Rattan Lal Hangloo of Hyderabad Central University, India; and many others for their insights need mention beyond all sincerity.

And finally it is you for whom **Taoshobuddha** will continue to overflow in myriad forms and his each breath pulsates for you. You are the seed that will certainly blossom as the **Flower of Enlightenment** one day. Therefore:

In the barren soils of thy inner sanctum
Oft do I use the manure of compassion?
Then one day seed of awakening I sow
With the rain of thy infinite bliss
The seed shall sprout one day
And then reckoning shall reap the fruits
At the dawn of new awakening!

LOVE YOU AND LOVE ALL!

Taoshobuddha

Email: mailtaoshobuddha@gmail.com
YOU TUBE. COM/ Taoshobuddha9
TOTAL BHAKTI.COM: ACCOUNT 'TAOSHOBUDDHA'
SCRIBD.COM: TAOSHOBUDDHACYBERLIBRARY
Issuu.com: TAOSHOBUDDHA
E. Book Mall.Com/Authors/Taoshobuddha
Doc Stoc.Com/Taoshobuddha

FOREWORD

DR. C. H. RAMNARINE MBBS
[MEDICAL PRACTITIONER ALTERNATIVE MEDICINE]

[Dr. C.H. Ramnarine popularly known as Harry is a renowned physician in Trinidad, whose light has spread to the wider communities in Canada, Caribbean Island, South America, and United States. A medical practitioner for 33 years, he has dedicated his time to ALTERNATE methods of healing. He is a blend of ancient techniques and the modern scientific techniques.]

I am very pleased to be given this opportunity by my good friend Brij Saksena—**TAOSHOBUDDHA** as you all call him, to write about the Author, his book, the quality of the audio and video meditations and the art of healing.

I fully agree with the author when he says, and the saying appears on the title of the book:

"Do not treat the disease, instead treat the patient!"

The disease and the patient are not separate. Sometimes disease comes to man other times he attracts the disease. But most of the time the disease and the man are one and the same. And unless you treat the patient healing cannot occur.

In thirty three years of medical practice I have followed this tenet in treating patients. As a medical practitioner I have found that allopathic medicine does not have answers for many questions that medical doctors have to face while examining and treating a patient. I have to seek alternative methods.

In my search over the years I have explored many methods and techniques like Aromatherapy, Flower Essences, Homeopathy, Ayurveda and other Native Healing Practices. I have explored almost all the possibilities to bring about inner health to the patients. This could not happen until all that impedes the process is removed. I agree that healing occurs when all these negative forces vanish; then the healing takes its natural course. As the author says health belongs to the fourth dimension. When disease symptoms are no more, something grows from within and this is known as **'HEALTH'.**

As the title **'MEDITATION THE ULTIMATE IN HEALING'** reflects, **the book is the outcome of the insights and deeper understanding of someone who has explored deep within an unfathomable treasure or reservoir. He has also a tremendous capacity to transfer such inner experiences to others as the process of healing.**

I have known the author for more than twenty years and found him to be an extraordinary human being. So I felt happy when he asked me to do the introduction to this book. **However, I was very impressed when I looked at the text and was even more so when I listened to the audio part of these meditations! I listened to them several times sometimes in deep meditation. My purpose was to analyze these audio and their role in healing.**

The various categories of body meditations, mind meditations, balancing the mind and meditation—the ultimate are all beautifully planned for the beginner as well as the experienced meditator.

The author refers to *breathing as the alphabet of the body.* It is an appropriate statement and a natural beginning of the process of healing! If one can correct the breathing many ailments vanish naturally.

Secondly, the selection of words, their arrangements, gaps between audio renditions, the background music and finally and most significantly the ability of the author through voice modulation to set the meditative tone. I found this ability to be spontaneous and natural with the author. *This clearly demonstrates his vast knowledge and experience in meditation.*

All these together create a total ambience for inner healing. **I have listened to these meditations to analyze the effects these create at various levels. I can certainly assure you that you cannot remain untouched by this.** *Together all these connect you to your being—the ultimate light that heals all.*

At times one may feel sleepy while listening to the audio but this is no ordinary sleep. It is not somnolence. This is the beginning of a connection first to your subconscious and then finally to your inner being.

Remember healing happens only when you are connected to your being. I quote the author:

"First, love gives you unity in your innermost core. Then you are no more a body, no more a mind, no more a soul.

You are simply one, unnamed, undefined and unclassified! You are no longer definable or comprehensible.

You simply become a mystery, a joy, a surprise, jubilation, and then a great celebration! A BEING, one with the whole! This is meditativeness. It is in such a state healing happens. I quote the author again:

'Meditation, on the other hand, considers man himself as a disease that comes to man because of inner imbalance between consciousness, ego, and mind and then disappears.'

What more can I say when the author has said *'MEDITATION THE ULTIMATE IN HEALING'. This is the Ultimate. Nothing is beyond this that I can say!*

I want to take you for a moment to the last chapter in the classic of the author's *MEDITATION, THE WAY TO SELF REALIZATION* this chapter entitled *MEDITATION AND HEALING*. When I asked the author about this his reply was this is just a beginning. I have yet to speak on **MEDITATION AND HEALING**. He was right then and now he has once again spoken as this work and continues to speak through many works for the process of inner healing to continue.

This book *MEDITATION THE ULTIMATE IN HEALING* is the answer and thus will continue the process of healing and insights of *TAOSHOBUDDHA.*

I recommend the book for anyone who seeks inner healing and deep insights into his Beingness.

Love!
DR. C.H.RAMNARINE
MBBS
Alternate Medicine Practitioner
ISHTARA CENTER TRINIDAD, W.I.

INTRODUCTION

A master can only help you in removing the
obstacles so that meditation happens!

MEDITATION THE WAY TO SELF REALIZATION-*Taoshobuddha—*
A STERLING PAPERBACK 2008

This morning as I woke up I found sun rose the same way. The chirping of the birds! And the rustling of the breeze across the Caribbean ocean was same. Yet still there is something new. The mind says everything is same—old. Not the being! For 'Being' life is ever new! Fresh! And alive too each finite moment! Eternity overflows through the finite moments. Only you have lost the contact.

The sun is new. Each day sun rises new. With a different luster! The birds chirp to bring the message of the unknown! Full of ecstasy! The breeze too is new and innocent! Do you know why?

Because it is a new dawn! A new dawn at the horizon! And also a dawn of new awakening! Just you and I! And bliss! A new surge of energy! A new silence surrounds!

And in a few moments I and you will be no more. Just the two beings will be overflowing! And aura of serenity and bliss!

This is why this morning is so unique and blissful! Drink this serenity to your heart's content. Only this much I can say! And let the silence do the rest!

For quite some time I was meaning to talk to you! And I was looking for you! Like a shadow for lives I have been following you. But you were always busy! It is only now that I got the opportunity. So let us go into an inner sojourn.

Your body is the visible soul. And soul is the invisible body. Body is manifest. And soul remains unmanifest. Both body and soul are part of one synergistic harmony.

Body and mind are the part of one organic whole. Accept your body. Love your body. The harmony that body creates will certainly become door to meditation one day. Love your body. Respect your body. Be grateful to your body.

Your body is the temple of the unknown. It is the most complex mechanism in the existence. Your body is not only unique it is marvelous as well.

Blessed are those who marvel.

Breathing is the alphabet of the body. And through breathing you can easily be bridged to meditation. Only you have to be aware of it. Be simply it! No thinking is needed! No feeling as well!

This is the ultimate experience of bliss! Beyond this there is nothing! This is eternal search! You have arrived home!

This is meditation!

Still you want to know more on meditation. How can you know God? The only way to know god, to feel god, and attain to godliness is meditation. Meditation means a state of consciousness when all thoughts have been dropped. The Zen masters call the state of meditation 'The Season of Autumn'. A season when all the leaves fall and the trees are standing bare, naked. So too when consciousness drops all thoughts it is like a tree without leaves! Without foliage! Simply exposed to the wind! To the moon! To the sun! And to the rain as well uncovered, unhidden. In that exposure there is communion with god. That communion is love. In that communion one becomes a beloved of god. Know this as meditativeness!

This is the taste of meditation!

This current work is an effort to harness the energy of being, words and mantras to create the energy field for transformation of human consciousness. And when you are transformed you enter the realm of the being! A blissful existence!

The autumn has arrived! In autumn the breeze is pleasantly cool, fresh, and rejuvenating! And when all the leaves have fallen and are fluttering, all those fallen yellow leaves create a golden atmosphere. They make even the wind golden! Although the wind remains uncolored yet still you can feel the song of the leaves! The dance of the leaves! The joy of the leaves and you can see the wind enjoying the whole dance. Such is the expression of inner joy that you feel surrounding you. This is the ultimate in meditation.

These twenty seven meditations are arranged in a sequence to harness the energies of the body and mind. And in the process these are balanced. Only then transformation can happen.

Do not find any meaning in these words. Otherwise you will move to the realm of the world and its dualities. Listen to these just as you listen to the roaring of the waves, or chirping of the birds. A new meaning will arise. Ummm . . .

SECTION 1

BODY MEDITATIONS

[1]

MEDITATION AND HEALING

[Reproduced: Meditation: The Way to Self Realization by Taoshobuddha, 2008, A Sterling Paperback, New Delhi, India]

Meditation is Ultimate in Healing

I t happened one day, when someone came to Buddha and enquired, "Who are you? Are you a philosopher or a thinker or a saint or a yogi?" Buddha responded, "I am only a healer, a Physician." So is each master. This is a beautiful reply—only a healer.

Man is a universe within an outer universe. Just like the body of the universe, the human body is composed of cells. These cells are interconnected by an electromagnetic force. This force works through electrolytes present in each cell. Individual human consciousness is a by-product of ego and mind. All States of pain and pleasure exist because of this ego-mind combination. It is because of this eternal pair of ego and mind that we have innumerable desires. Man requires tremendous energy to fulfill these desires. Unfulfilled desires cause illness and pain. This requires methods to cure disease and pain.

Instead of saying, man gets sick or diseased, it will be better to say that disease comes to man. Or more precisely, man invites diseases as an inter-play of trinity—Consciousness, Ego, and Mind. In addition to this, man is a disease. This is his problem as well as uniqueness. This is his misfortune and his good fortune as well.

Except man, no other creature on earth has such problems as anxiety, tension, disease, and illness the way man has. Because of all this, man has evolved and attained growth. Disease means, man cannot be. Also, man has not accepted what he is. He is not happy where he is. This is man's dynamism, his restlessness, and at the same times his misfortune as well. It is so because man is agitated and unhappy and is therefore suffering.

Except man, no other creature has the capability to go mad. No animal goes insane on its own, unless man drives him mad. In the forest no animal is mad. However, when an animal comes in contact with man, it becomes perverted. Animals get perverted in the zoo in the association of man. Also, no animal commits suicide but man does.

For this, two methods have been invented and used. These two methods are medicine and meditation. These are two extremes. Out of the combination of the two, many possibilities have emerged. Both these systems provide treatment for the same disease with multiple possibilities.

It is significant to know the understanding of each system as far as treatment is concerned. Medicine considers each disease in man separately. This is the approach that analyzes disease as a part. Meditation, on the other hand, considers man himself as a disease that comes to man because of inner imbalance between consciousness, ego, and mind and then disappears. And thus considers the very personality of man as disease. Medicine considers disease as alien to man. However, this trend is now changing and even medical science has started saying, do not treat the disease, and instead treat the patient.

"Do not treat the disease, instead treat the patient," is a very significant statement. This implies that disease is nothing but a way of life, and a patient understands his life, and thus lives the life. No too men fall sick the same way. In fact diseases have their own individualities. It is not that if two persons suffer from a particular disease, the two patients will definitely be of the same kind, and need the same treatment. The two individuals have a different anatomy, physiology, and psychology as well. It may also happen that the treatment for the same disease for two different individuals will certainly be different. Thus deep down, the individuality of the patient is the root, not the disease.

Both medicine and meditation follow a different approach to understand the cause of the disease. And thus, differ significantly in the treatment and the healing process. Medicine treats the disease in a very superficial way. Here one thing has to be kept in mind, that by medicine I mean regular medicine not the alternative one. Meditation gets hold of man from deep within. In other words it can be said, that medicine attempts to bring about health to a person from outside and meditation attempts to keep the inner being of the person healthy. However, there is a deep inter-relation between the two approaches. Neither can the science of medicine nor the science of meditation be complete without the other. Remember, man is both body and soul. And that which connects the two is consciousness and the mind.

For thousands of years man has considered that the body and the soul of a person are two separate entities. Such understanding brought about two dangerous results. One group considered man as soul alone and thus, the body was negated. This approach brought about development in the meditative way of life and understanding.

Medicine was thus neglected and it could not become a science in the hands of meditators. The body was totally disregarded. On the contrary, the other approach considered man as body alone and thus neglected the soul. And as a result of this tremendous research and development brought about advancements in medicine! In this process meditation was first negated completely and then as a result of this negation it was neglected out rightly.

Man is both body and soul. The body comes into existence through the interaction between an ovum and sperm. This can be proved scientifically and understood as well. However, 'what' enters the body is a phenomenon beyond human understanding. No one has seen, only imagined, that which enters the body and how.

When I say man is both body and soul simultaneously, it creates a linguistic mistake. Saying so, gives an impression that these two things are separate from one another yet still interconnected. However, in fact, the body and mind are two sides of the same coin or two ends of one pole. If this be true, then we cannot say that man is body plus soul. Instead, man is psychosomatic. Man is mind-body or body-mind mechanism.

In reality, the body is gross. It is that part of the soul that falls within the grasp of our senses. And the soul is that part of the body that lies beyond the comprehension of senses. The soul is the invisible body, and the body is the visible soul. The two are not separate. Instead, they are two different states of vibration of the same reality.

And this duality has been harmful for mankind. A dualistic mind always thinks in terms of two. This creates problems. Earlier we considered matter and energy as separate. This perspective has now changed. Now we say matter is energy. Matter and energy are two different forms of the same energy. So too, the human body and soul are two ends of the same entity!

We can say the body and soul are two ends or gateways for illness to come in. Illness can come in from the door of the body and then spread to the soul. In fact, whatever happens to the body, its vibrations reach the soul. This is the reason behind the fact that, sometimes patients are cured physically and yet they keep feeling ill. The disease has left the body and the doctors say that the patient is cured, but the patient still feels ill and refuses to believe that he is not sick. Various pathological tests indicate that clinically everything is alright. Yet the patient still feels unwell.

Such patients create problems for the doctor, because all modes of known investigations indicate that there is no disease. And having no disease does not mean that you are healthy. Health has its own positive attitude. Health belongs to the dimensionless dimension. Health is not the absence of disease. This is a negative state. One can say there is no thorn, but this does not indicate the presence of the flower. The absence of thorns is one thing and the presence of the flower is another thing.

The science of medicine has not been able to achieve anything positive as far as health is concerned. The entire medical field is concerned with the nature of diseases and finding ways and means to eradicate the symptoms of these diseases. It is considered that the absence of disease leads to health.

Medical science can easily define disease in definitions and symptoms but when it comes to health, it tries to deceive you. It says, when there is no disease, and then whatever remains is health. This is not the definition of health. It is like defining a flower in relation to thorns. No science of medicine has been able to say what health is. It can only say something about disease. There is a reason for it. The science can only grasp the outer bodily manifestations. From outside only disease can be grasped. Health can only be grasped from what is within the man—his innermost being.

The Hindi equivalent for health is *'Swasthya.'* It is really a beautiful word. However, health is not synonymous with **Swasthya.** Health comes from healing and therefore, it is related to illness. Health implies healing of the symptoms. One has recovered and thus the healing has happened. The difference between these two words indicates two different origins and approaches, and also the understanding of those who coined these words.

However, **Swasthya** does not indicate this. It actually implies one who has settled within himself. One who has reached his inner core! **Swasthya** means, the one who has understood the very essence of existence. This is the reason **Swasthya** cannot be synonymous with health. In fact, there is no word in any language that comes closer to **Swasthya**. The very word **Swasthya** indicates there is no physical, emotional, or psychological illness within. This is necessary but is not enough for **Swasthya**. Something else is also needed. This comes from the other end of the pole—from your being. It does not matter if the disease begins from the outer source. Its vibrations are echoed in the soul.

It is like throwing a stone in the tranquil waters of the lake. The disturbance occurs at the spot where the stone was thrown but the ripples that are produced reach even the banks. In fact, the ripples reach every corner even where the stone did not reach. All that happens to the body too; its ripples, as echo, reach the innermost core.

Therefore, when a man falls ill, vibrations of the disease enter the realm of the soul. This is the reason that illness still persists even after the body has been treated. This continuation of the sickness is because of its vibrations that are echoing all the way to the innermost being. For this, medical science has no answer.

Therefore, medical science will always remain incomplete, without the dimension of meditation and the understanding that comes when meditation happens. Of course, it is in the interest of the doctors that patients not be cured and only the disease is cured. When this happens, the patients keep coming back again and again and thus the business continues.

A disease can also begin from the other end. Actually, in the state in which man is, disease is already present. Man is plagued with tension. Except man, no other creature is diseased this way. Man wants to become what he is not. This creates tension. No other creature has this idea. A dog is a dog. A monkey is a monkey. No animal is seeking to become other than what they are. But a man has to become a human being, which he is not yet. We can never say that a dog is a less dog. All dogs are dogs, equally. They are living in their essential nature. It is only man who is not living in his nature. He is not happy with himself. So he constantly strives to be that which he is not. In doing so he forgets what he was really meant to be. Man is never born in his completeness or totality.

His is in an incomplete state. All other animals are born complete. This is not so with man. He has to do certain things to be total. This state of incompleteness is his disease. This is the reason that man is troubled twenty-four hours. And it is not that only the poor are in trouble. This is how we generally think. We do not realize that on becoming rich, troubles do not vanish, only their level and form changes.

The truth is that a poor man never has the amount of anxiety that the rich man has. The poor man, at least, has a justification for his problems. But the rich man does not have even this justification. He cannot pinpoint the reason for his anxiety. And when the anxiety is without any visible reason, it multiplies. When you have the reason, it gives you some consolation and relief. In that case, there is hope that the reasons can be removed. But, when some trouble arises without any reason, then the difficulty increases.

It is interesting to know that there was a time when the masters were doctors. It will not be surprising when a time comes, when once again the masters and the doctors will be the same. This has started already, because for the first time it has become clear that the question is not that of the body alone.

It has also come to light that if the body is healthy, the problems increase manifold. It is so because, for the first time the person starts sensing the disease which is within, at the other end of the body—the invisible end!

We tend to feel something only when there is problem. You feel your leg only when there is a problem. Without the problem, you remain oblivious of that part. When the thorn is in the leg, then your whole being becomes like an arrow, pointing towards the leg. In that case, it only becomes aware of the leg. When the thorn is removed from the leg, then the being has to shift its attention and then will notice something else as well.

Medicine tries to free man from disease—superfluously, at the level of the body. Remember, even when you are freed from illness, you are not free from the basic disease of being a man. The disease of being a man is the desire for the impossible. This disease cannot be satisfied with anything. This makes every achievement futile. Also, it attaches significance to whatever one does not have.

Meditation is the cure for the disease that man is. For all other diseases, physicians have a cure. However, for the disease of being man, only meditation is the cure. Medical science will be complete the day we understand this inner side of man and start working with that too.

I did mention earlier that whenever the body becomes ill, the vibrations and the ripples are felt in the soul as well. And when the soul is diseased, then the ripples reach the body.

It is because of this, there are so many types of 'pathies' in the world. This should not be so, if pathology is a science, and then there cannot be so many pathies. It is relevant because man's disease is manifold. Certain diseases cannot be cured with allopathy. In case of diseases, which originate from within and then travel to the outside, allopathy is useless. For the diseases that start from the outside and move into the interior, allopathy is very successful. Diseases that reach the outside from within are not bodily diseases. They simply manifest on the bodily plane. They are psychic or still deeper, spiritual ones.

If a person is suffering from a disease in his psyche, this implies, no clinical medicine can give him any relief. It will be harmful to administer medicine to him because the medicine will try to do something, and in the process if it does not provide relief, it is bound to do harm. Medicines like homeopathy could be administered, that do not harm anyone; but there is no question of relief either. They are incapable of giving any relief, but this does not mean that people do not get relief.

Remember, to get relief is an entirely different matter; so too, to give relief is also a different matter. These are two different phenomena. People do get relief if the disease is at the level of their psyche. In that case they need some placebo for it. They need some consolation or an assurance that they are not sick. They simply carry the idea that they are sick.

This has led to many illusory medicines or placebos. When ten patients are suffering from the same disease and three of them are treated through allopathy, three through homeopathy, and three through naturopathy, then an interesting result is obtained. Each of these pathies is effective to a certain degree.

My own understanding is that, allopathy is the only scientific medicine. However, there is something unscientific in man that scientific medicine alone will not do. Allopathy alone deals with the human body in a very scientific and systematic manner. However, it cannot cure hundred percent, because man in his inner being is imaginative, inventive, and projective as well. Actually, it is due to some unscientific reason when allopathy does not work on a person. You may wonder what it means to be sick due to unscientific reasons.

The word unscientific may sound very strange. You know of the scientific system of treatment and the unscientific system as well. So too, you can have scientific sickness as well as unscientific sickness. All the diseases that start at the psyche of a person and manifest at the level of the body, cannot be cured in a scientific manner.

We consider only one side of man. Then we go on eliminating the diseases that originate from the mind. And as such their number is increasing. And now, even those who think only in terms of science have started agreeing that at least fifty percent of diseases arise due to the mind. This is not so in India and other parts of the east, because for the diseases of the mind, a strong mind is needed! In the west the number of such diseases is increasing.

All such diseases usually begin from within and then spread to the outside. These are outgoing diseases. If you try to treat the bodily manifestation of such diseases, then it will find another way to manifest. It will manifest from the weakest link of your personality. This is the reason that many times physicians are not only able to treat the disease but are also responsible for multiplying the various forms of the disease.

I knew a young girl who loved someone very dearly. However, her parents did not allow her to marry that person. She lost all desire to see anyone else. She got blind! Even the eye specialists could not find anything wrong with her eyes. It was concluded that she was deceiving. When I enquired from her, during our conversation, it was revealed that she had no desire to see anyone else if she could not see her lover. She became psychologically blind. Such things happen quite often. This cannot be diagnosed through the anatomy of the eyes, because the anatomy is normal. And the mechanism of seeing is functional. This was her way of committing suicide.

Another person I knew developed throat cancer. His eldest son had a scientific mind. He would not allow his father to visit any doctor. In that city there was another physician, who was not trained in regular medicine. When he saw the patient, he said his cancer was due to cockroaches. And it was observed that each time the bed was made up during the day, there were cockroaches under his pillow and the sheet as well. Even if the bed was made just an hour ago! The physician prescribed some treatment and assured him that within seven days' time he would come to visit him, by himself. However, it was not the case to be. His eldest son did not allow him this treatment, even against the wishes of his mother. This resulted in the death of the person.

Mystically, I assure you, meditation is the cure at the other end of the human being. By meditation I do not mean a Hindu meditation or Christian meditation or any other brand of meditation. Meditation is just the technique to change the energy patterns. Naturally, medicines depend on matter and their chemical constituents, while meditation depends on consciousness.

There are no tablets available for meditation, though many efforts are being made to produce the medicine for meditation. But this cannot be done. Actually, this is in keeping with the same old stubbornness of only treating from the level of the body—all outside treatments. We cannot reach the innermost being through chemical means. The deeper we go inside, the less will be the effect of the chemicals. The deeper we go within man, the less meaningful the physical and material approach starts becoming.

Because of prejudices, this has not been achieved. Interestingly, medicine is one of the two or three most orthodox professions in the world. Medical professors and doctors are listed among the most orthodox people. They are not able to let go of the old idea and accept that something else can also actually cure the patient. The reason is quite natural. If the doctors drop the old idea and become flexible, then they will have a difficult time teaching the children. If the things are fixed, then there will be efficiency. So the ideas must be definite and solid. This will bring confidence.

Even a criminal does not require as much confidence as a professor does. He has to be self-confidant that whatever he is saying is absolutely right. This makes the person orthodox. Teachers become orthodox. This is harmful, because in reality, education needs to be the least orthodox, otherwise it will create obstacles in the way of progress. This is the reason why there is no teacher who is also an inventor. There are so many professors in the universities, world over but the inventions and discoveries are all made by people outside these universities. More than seventy percent of Nobel Prize winners are people outside the universities.

Medicine is another profession full of orthodoxy, though there is a professional reason for it. Doctors have to take quick decisions, and if they start contemplating when the patient is on the deathbed, then only the ideas will remain and not the patient. If the doctor is unorthodox, liberal, and practices new theories or does new experiments each time, then there is danger. He has to take instant decisions. All such people rely on past experiences and information. This is the reason that the medical profession runs almost thirty years behind medical research.

This results in many patients dying unnecessarily and untimely as well! What actually happens is that, that which should not be being practiced today, is actually being followed. This is a professional hazard, and some of the concepts of the doctors deep down are very fundamentalist. One of them is their faith in medicine more than in man himself—more faith in chemicals than in the consciousness. More importance is being given to chemistry as compared to consciousness. The most dangerous outcome of this attitude is that, while chemistry is being given more importance, no experiments are being done on consciousness.

Let me give you a few examples to bring home the point. Trying to have a painless labor during childbirth is an age old problem. Of course, the priests are against this. In fact, the priests are against the very idea that the world should be free from pain and suffering. If this be so, then they will lose their ground. In that case, their profession will have no meaning. When there is suffering, pain, or sickness, then we say a prayer or do Yajna or perform some other ritual. If there is no suffering, then people may even forget God. We remember God only in suffering. Priests have always been against painless labor. They say that the pain during labor is natural.

Even, to call it an arrangement of God is false. No God wants the mother to have a painful childbirth. The doctors believe that for painless birth, some medicines have to be administered. Some chemicals, like anesthesia should be given. All these remedies begin at the level of the body. This implies, getting the body in such a state that the mother does not realize that she is in pain. Naturally, women themselves have been experimenting with this on their own for centuries.

It is significant to note, that nearly seventy-five percent of the babies are born during the night. During the daytime, it is difficult because a woman is very active and aware of the time. When the woman is asleep, she is more relaxed and it is easier for the baby to be born. So, nearly seventy-five percent babies are born in the darkness of the night! In fact, the mother starts creating obstacles for the child, right from the moment it is to be born. Of course, later on she manages so many obstacles for the child, but she begins causing hindrances for the child even before the child is born.

One of the remedies is, to do something through medication to relax the body. These remedies are being followed, but these are not free from drawbacks. The biggest drawback is that we do not, at all, consider the consciousness of the person. Also, the trust in human consciousness goes on decreasing. And thus, consciousness disappears.

A doctor, named Dr. Fernand Lamaze, has trusted the human consciousness, and thus, he has managed thousands of painless deliveries of babies. This is the method of conscious cooperation. Accordingly, the mother cooperates immediately and consciously during delivery. She welcomes this. There is no fight against it. There is no resistance. The pain that a mother encounters is not due to childbirth but because of the fight. Due to the fight, she tries to constrict the whole mechanism of childbirth. There is a constant fear of pain. This makes her afraid of labor. The fear arising due to resistance prevents the child from being born. This pain is not natural. It arises only because of resistance.

Two solutions are there to solve this problem of resistance. We can sedate the mother. This happens at the level of the body. Remember one thing, that a mother who delivers the child in a state of unconsciousness can never become a mother in the fullest sense. There is a reason for this. With the birth of the child, not only is the child born, but the mother is also born. With childbirth two things happen. The child is born and also an ordinary woman becomes a mother. But when the child is born in a state of unconsciousness, the basic relationship between the mother and the child is distorted. In this process, the mother is not born. And thus, she is only reduced to a nurse.

I am not in favor of delivering the child by sedating the mother, with the help of a chemical or using artificial means. The mother should be fully conscious during delivery. In that very consciousness, the mother is also born. If you realize the truth of this matter, it will mean that the mother's consciousness should be trained for delivery. In fact, the mother should undergo childbirth meditatively.

Meditation has two meanings for the mother. One is that, she should not resist. She should cooperate with whatever is going on. Just like a river flows whenever there is depression in the earth, just as the winds are blowing, just as the dry leaves are falling—no one gets even the slightest inkling of it and dry leaves continue falling—so too, she should be in total cooperation during her delivery. Be fully meditative in the event. This will lead to painless childbirth. I am speaking of this on the basis of scientific evidences. Many experiments have been done using this method. Lamaze is one such method of painless childbirth.

To begin this process, we need to start harboring an ill feeling towards the person or the thing that produces pain in us from the very first contact. Naturally you fall into a sort of enmity with the person with whom you encounter a struggle in our first experience. This becomes an obstacle in forming a friendly relationship. You cannot create the bridge of cooperation with the person with whom we develop conflict.

It is interesting to know that we have, so far, only heard of labor pain, and never heard of 'labor bliss'. This has not yet happened. However, with full cooperation, labor bliss is bound to happen. I am in favor of such blissful birth. With the help of medical science we can experience a blissful birth, instead of a painless birth. So when we approach from the side of consciousness, we can certainly create a blissful birth. Then, we can create a conscious inner connection between the mother and the child. This was an example, to put across to you, that some things can be done from within as well.

When it comes to sickness, we try to treat it only from the outside. This leads us to a question: Is the patient really ready from inside, to cure himself? We never bother to find this. It may be quite possible that the disease is self-invited, and the number of such self-invited sicknesses is many. Actually, very few diseases come of their own accord. Most of them are self-invited. We invite them long before they actually come. As a result, we do not see any connection between the cause and effect.

For thousands of years in societies world over, we could not see any connection between physical intercourse and childbirth. The gap is that of nine months. It becomes difficult to relate to such a distant cause and effect and then, not all intercourses lead to childbirth. Obviously, there is no reason to connect the cause and effect. It was only much later that man understood, that what had happened nine months back was resulting in childbirth now. Such is the cause and effect relationship. Something like this happens in relation to sickness too. Very often we invite the sickness. But it comes much later. Too much time has flowed between the two events.

I can go on citing examples in this regards. But that will not serve the purpose of this book. Therefore, I will resist myself.

Man has not yet developed a compassionate attitude towards such mind-oriented diseases. If my leg is hurt, then everyone will be sympathetic, but if my mind is hurt, then it will be a mental disease. It will be as if I have definitely done something wrong. For all mind-oriented diseases the person is blamed, while it is not his fault!

All mind-oriented diseases have their own place, but physicians do not accept this. This is because, there is treatment only for body-oriented diseases, and all mind-oriented diseases are beyond this understanding.

So the physicians do not consider these as diseases. This requires a different doctor and a different line of treatment as well. His treatment has to begin from within and then move outwards.

Meditation is the treatment that moves from inside out.

It happened, that one day someone came to Buddha and enquired, "Who are you? Are you a philosopher, or a thinker, or a saint, or a yogi?" Buddha responded, "I am only a healer, a physician." So is each master. This is a beautiful reply—only a healer.

I know something about the inner. I romanced with meditation. So this is what is overflowing, like the Whispers of the Unknown now.

The day man can understand that there is something to be done about these mind-oriented diseases—because we will not be able to cure all body-oriented diseases completely—that day we will realize that both science and religion are two approaches to explore that which is. That day both medicine and meditation will be closer. It is only medicine that can, really, bridge this gap between medicine and meditation. No other science can bridge the gap.

Neither chemistry, nor physics, nor mathematics can come closer to religion. Mathematics can survive even without religion. However, in no way will mathematics need help from religion. It can develop on its own. Mathematics is only a game. It is not for life.

A doctor is not playing any game. Medicine deals with life. It is the doctor who has the capability to be the bridge between science and meditation. This has now started happening to some extent, but only in more developed and understanding nations. This is so because the doctors deal with life! This is what Carl Gustav Jung said, just before dying. He said that, on the basis of being a physician, I can say that all the patients who come to me after the age of forty, basically their illnesses are because of the lack of religion. It is quite surprising. But if somehow we can give them some kind of religion, then they will become healthy.

Let's try and understand this. Up to the age of thirty-five the body is on the rise. However, after forty it begins to move downwards. It may be true, that up to thirty-five years one may not need meditation or find any value in meditation because he is body-oriented. The body is still on the rise. Up to this stage all diseases are body-oriented. After the age of thirty-five years, perhaps all diseases take a new turn. Now, life has begun to move towards the other pole of life—death. So when life grows, it spreads towards the outside. And when man dies, he shrinks within.

The truth is that, most probably, all diseases of the old people are deep rooted in death. Usually it is said, that the concerned person died because of a specific sickness. It will be better to say that the concerned person is sick because of death. It is the fear and the possibility of death that makes a person vulnerable to all kinds of diseases. So as soon as a person feels that he is moving towards death all doors to various diseases are open.

Even if a healthy person comes to know for sure that he is going to die tomorrow, he will certainly fall sick. Everything was alright. All the reports were normal. X-ray was normal. The blood pressure was within normal limits, the pulse was normal, the stethoscope was conveying that everything was perfect. However, if a person becomes convinced completely that tomorrow he is going to die then, you will find that he is catching a variety of diseases. He will catch so many diseases within twenty-four hours that he cannot catch them even in twenty-four lives.

What has really happened to this person? He has, in fact, opened himself up to all kinds of diseases. He has stopped resisting. He is sure of death approaching or knocking the door of his consciousness. He has moved away from his consciousness, which was acting as a wall within him. Now he is ready for death, so the diseases have started coming in. This is the reason that a retired person dies soon.

Often it is enquired, what happens when the consciousness of a person becomes healthy from within? First it happens when he starts feeling his consciousness within. By nature we feel only the body—like our hands, feet etc. There is no feeling of 'I am'. Human awareness is centered on the house, not on the one who really lives within.

This is a very difficult situation. If the house starts falling apart, then man begins to think that he is falling apart. This, in fact, becomes the sickness. However, when you understand that you are different from the house and, in fact, it is you, who is living within, you understand that even if the body falls apart you will still remain. This makes the difference. Then the fear of death vanishes.

However, the fear of death can never disappear. Meditation is, therefore, the awareness of oneself. Human consciousness is always aware about something but never about itself. This is the reason that when you are sitting alone you feel sleepy, because there is nothing to do. When you do not see anything, there is darkness around and you fall asleep. Remember, both sleep and meditation resemble in one way but are different in another. Sleep means, you are all alone and you are in slumber. In meditation too, you are all alone but you are awake.

It so happened that, once a king named Prasanjit came to meet Buddha! He was expecting a kingly welcome. But that was not so. He felt embarrassed. So, when he was sitting in front of Buddha, his big toe was shaking and he was fidgety. Seeing this the Buddha asked, "Why is your toe shaking?"

At this, the person replied, "Forget it. It was just shaking. And I was not even aware of it."

Buddha said, "Your toe is shaking and you are not even aware of it. Whose toe is this? Is it your toe?"

The King replied, "Yes indeed, the toe is mine. But why are you deviating? You continue the sermon."

Buddha responded, "I cannot continue because the person I was talking to is unconscious. So remain aware of your toe movement in future. Such things will multiply your awareness. Because out of the awareness of the toe, will evolve the awareness of the watcher as well."

Remember, awareness is a double-pointed arrow. If you experiment with it, then one side of awareness will face outwards and the other will pierce within you. So basically, meditation leads to the awareness of our body and our being. When this awareness increases, the fear of death will wither away.

So if medical science cannot remove this fear of death, it can never cure this disease that man is! Medical science tries to expand the life span. But increasing the life span really increases the waiting period for death. It is better for the waiting period to be shorter.

Meditation is the realization of this immortality. It is the experience that, which is within never dies and is never born. This is the reason you should treat the body medically, so that it can live happily as long as it lives. At the same time, try to be aware of that which is within, so that when death is at your doorstep you are not afraid! This inner understanding is fearlessness.

Meditation from within and medication from the outside can complement medical science as a complete science! In fact, both meditation and medicine are two poles of the same science. However, the link is missing, but these are coming closer. Now in most of the major hospitals, a hypnotist is essential. However, hypnotism is not meditation, instead, it is a stepping stone.

It shows that there is the need for something to be done with the consciousness of man. This is an important step. Today a hypnotist has entered the hospital, and then tomorrow a religious place can enter and then we can expect a separate department for meditation and yoga! Only then we can cure the person as a whole. Medicine will take care of the body. Psychology will take care of the mind, and yoga and meditation will take care of the soul.

Thus, comes in the concept of soul healing. And also the Soul Mind Body Medicine!

The human body and its immune system have tremendous healing qualities. When your finger is cut, it will heal by itself even without any treatment. Your cold gets cured in a few days. Even a fracture can heal by itself. Thus, Soul Mind Body medicine works with the body's inherent healing qualities. It expands and deepens the potential of your body itself, by focusing on the soul as the master healer.

The soul has incredible healing power! But the soul of your body is not the only soul whose power you can tap. Every bodily system has a soul, as does every organ, every cell, and every strand of DNA and RNA.

In addition, there are numerous outer souls—the animals, oceans, mountains, trees, flowers, buildings, earth, other planets, the sun, the moon, the stars, and the galaxies—all have souls. In fact, everything; even the words have soul and all these have incredible healing capabilities. You have to learn the capabilities of Soul Mind Body.

Heal the soul first, and then healing of the mind and body will follow. Meditation from within and medication from the outside can complement medical science as a complete science! In fact, both meditation and medicine are two poles of the same science. However, the link is missing.

The day man can understand that there is something to be done about these mind-oriented diseases—because we will not be able to cure all body-oriented diseases completely—that day we will realize that both science and religion are two approaches to explore that which is. That day both medicine and meditation will be closer. It is only medicine that can, really, bridge this gap between medicine and meditation. No other science can bridge the gap. Medicine deals with life. It is the doctor who has the capability to be the bridge between science and meditation.

[2]

BREATHING THE ALPHABET

BREATH IS LIFE! BREATH IS PRANA!
THE ESSENTIAL LIFE FORCE!
BE AWARE OF BREATHING!

Observe your incoming and outgoing breath. Continue to observe your breathing. Each moment breath comes in and then goes out. Flow with the music as its rhythm stills something within.

Music flows on . . .

As you begin to observe your incoming and outgoing breath breathing slows down. You go on witnessing the breath. First it slows and then it settles. And then . . . Inner rhythm overflows as music . . .

And with the settling of the breath all vibrations cease as well. Not only has this, also something settles deep within. Breath continues rhythmically both in and out!

Flow with the rhythm of the music as it creates ripple within . . .

Still the vibration of body continues. Also continues the one who witnesses this all—the subtle one. As witnessing continues you enter into another realm. This is the realm of consciousness that witnesses all this!

Flow with existence . . .

Something stills within! Yet still there continues the vibrations of thoughts. This continues like the vibration of breath. The witness and the vibration of breath continue.

Flow with life as it unveils . . .

The subtle witness of the breath continues. There are many other vibrations that continue as well. These are the vibrations of thoughts.

Flow with being . . .

Thoughts flow on the inner sky like the crowd on a busy place. This is like the crowd in a busy place. People coming and going! So too thoughts continue to float on the inner sky.

Allow the life to flow within . . .

Between these thoughts there is a gap! The gap between two thoughts is precise. The gap between two passersby is the way to be aware of the gap between the two thoughts . . .

Feel the stillness within . . .

Beyond all vibrations is your **Chaitanya** or conscious form! No form is deeper than this. Like the ocean is the realm of this stillness. Out of this flows silence in this total stillness. And you get the taste of your being!

Allow the music to sink deep within . . .

In this you experience your presence! In action worldly experiences him. In action and in movement alone a worldly experiences his presence. And the meditator experiences him in this stillness. Meditation is the process to experience you in this utter stillness.

Still flow with music . . .

Breath is silent. Thoughts have ceased. Only being is there. Take a few deep breaths! Raise your hand towards the sky. And be filled with gratitude. Such are the moments of inner drowning! Myriad gratitude for this!

Allow to drown still deeper within . . .

To experience your being in a state of inactivity, inaction and thoughtlessness is meditation. A few deep breaths! Raise your hand above head towards the sky in gratitude that you have such moments to drown in yourself. And gently stand and celebrate the gratitude! And allow it to disseminate in the outer atmosphere! Also allow it to surround you each finite moment a new meaning will arise. Such is new beginning, new life, and new living. This is Alpha in meditation. With Alpha Omega is not far.

This is the taste of your being!

[3]

BODY IS THE TEMPLE

One simply is. One is not doing anything.
No thinking. No one is feeling anything.
This ishness is the Ultimate Experience of bliss!
Beyond this there is nothing!
This is eternal search.
You have arrived home. This is Meditation!

MEDITATION: THE WAY TO SELF REALIZATION—TAOSHOBUDDHA

Your body is manifest creation. And soul is the unmanifest creation. Body is visible. And soul is invisible and unmanifest. Both visible and invisible stay together. It is the harmony of the manifest and unmanifest that creates inner balance. And inner balance manifests itself in the outer realm.

Out of this inner balance wafts the fragrance of the being or soul. You can be this fragrance. And then something will spring forth from within.

Both body and the soul are the part of one harmony. They are the part of one whole.

Out of the whole evolves the whole. Qualitatively, just as both drop and the ocean are same so too is the whole and that evolves out of the whole.

पूर्णमदः पूर्णमिदं पूर्णात् पूर्ण मुदच्यते ।
पूर्णस्य पूर्णमादाय पूर्ण मेवा व शिष्यते ॥

Totality alone is. Feel it within.
Feel its harmony! And its rhythm as well!

Accept the body. Love your body. Respect it. And be grateful to it. Body is the most complex mechanism in existence. It is simply marvelous.

Begin with a feeling of AWE! And Wonder! With your body and its mechanism! Body is closest. You know this. This you can feel and touch as well. So begin with that which is closer to you.

Through the body existence has come closest to you. Through your body God has approached you.

Your body contains the water of the oceans! Fire of the stars and the sun as well! As life force or 'Prana Vayu' air constitutes your body. Your body is made of earth.

Your body represents all the elements of which existence is composed of. What a transformation! What a metamorphosis! Look at the earth and now look at your body. What a transformation! And you have never marveled.

Dust has become divine. What greater mystery can there be? What greater miracle can there be? This you cannot envision. You are only interested in petty miracles.

Each finite moment existence happens as miracle. A speck of dust becomes divine as your body. Out of mud blossoms the divine beauty as a flower. A dew drop slips from the lotus leaf to dissolve in the lake.

Out of mud has evolved your beautiful body.

This is the miracles of the unknown. Be open to this. Open your eyes to witness this. A new vision awaits thee!!!

MEDITATION IS ULTIMATE FLOWERING!

[4]

WISDOM OF THE BODY

When you are one, suddenly you see this oneness outside. All barriers vanish. There is no 'I', no 'Thou'. There is only god or truth or Samadhi or whatever you may call this. You may even call this nirvana. Zen calls this Sonoma or Konomama. This is pure Ishness! Also this is suchness or what Buddha calls as Thathata.

MEDITATION THE WAY TO SELF REALIZATION: 2008

You are the miracle of the unknown! This you have forgotten. This is the cause of your misery! And disease too! I am therefore the reminder!

Wisdom is wisdom. Wisdom is truth. Wisdom is eternal. Wisdom is the growth of consciousness within. Wisdom that falls from its realm to the level of the listener is knowledge. Wisdom is an experience. It is evolution. Wisdom brings innocence.

A totally different kind of wisdom is needed. A wisdom where you can hear the whispers of the unknown? A different kind of education in the world is needed. I introduce you to the silence of the heart.

What is this silence of your heart? Know this as Meditation. Names matter not. What is more important is the essence of it?

27

Meditation begins with you. Be compassionate to your body. Why? It is the miracle of the Unknown. It is the temple of the being. Therein dwells the shrine of the being.

Begin with being compassionate to your body. Unless you are compassionate to your body you cannot be compassionate to the other.

Your body is living organism. It has done no harm to you. It is continuously in your service. Since conception it has been serving you. And will continue to do so until the death comes. For you it will go on doing anything. Even the impossible! It has never disobeyed you.

You cannot conceive of any mechanism so wise and obedient. You will be amazed if you know all that your body is doing for you. This is miraculous and mysterious. But you are blind to this. You are not acquainted with your own body. But you go on pretending that you love others.

Your body is the greatest mystery in the existence. You have to love this mystery. You have to love its mysteries and its functioning as well.

Unfortunately all religions and philosophers are against body. Body is considered lowest. There is definite reason. If you learn the wisdom of the body you will not need religious preceptors. Then you would have uncovered the greatest mystery within.

You are body. You are mind. And also you are something beyond these two as well. This you know not. Body is gross. To know the gross no intelligence is needed. To know body no meditation is needed. Mind is relatively subtle. Yet still you can get slight glimpse of the mind as well. It is so because mind is between gross and the subtle. Mind is connected both to the body and the soul as well. From the side of the body you do sometimes get the glimpse of the mind. But you never get a glimpse of the soul. To 'you' the soul appears to be an empty word that is meaningless. When you hear the word soul no ripples arise in you. This word creates restlessness in you.

And within the mystery of the body is the shrine of consciousness. You are the essence of consciousness.

You . . . are the essence . . . of consciousness . . . Ummm!!!

[5]

ESSENCE OF CONSCIOUSNESS!!

One simply is. One is not doing anything.
No thinking. No one is feeling anything.
This ishness is the ultimate experience of bliss!
Beyond this there is nothing! This is eternal search.
You have arrived home. This is meditation!

MEDITATION: THE WAY TO SELF REALIZATION—2008

You are the essence of consciousness. Be aware of this. Be aware you are the essence of consciousness. Consciousness is your being. This is God within. There is no God above you. Only such a person can be respectful towards other human beings. Not only that, instead towards other living beings as well! The entire existence is as mysterious as you are. Only expressions and variety differs. This makes life richer.

Once you have found the consciousness within. You have discovered the key to ultimate within.

Education that does not teach you to love your body! Or teach you to be compassionate to your body! And does not teach you to enter its mysteries! Will not be able to teach you to enter your own consciousness!

The body is the door to the unknown. The stepping stone! Any education that does not touch the subject of body and the consciousness remains incomplete. Not only that, it is dangerous as well.

It is the flowering of consciousness that can prevent you from any destruction. Consciousness gives you an urge and impetus to create. Create more beauty! And comfort!

You need a healthier body! A better body! You need a more conscious and alert being!

Existence is ready to give you paradise here now. Life is here now. Life is paradise. But you go on postponing paradise till after death.

Tomorrow never comes. Life is here now. Life is celebration. Life is bliss. Life is a song. Life is a dance of consciousness. If you can live your life like this you are paradise. If you can live life like this no death can take away the serenity and the bliss of the being.

I teach you this paradise. I teach you to choose happiness each finite moment. Life is bliss. Happiness is your choice. Happiness is not a condition. No discipline is needed to love. Lovingness is the fragrance of your being. And to be happy is the quality of the being.

A little awareness! A little understanding is needed. Know this as the wisdom of the body. Consciousness is the wisdom of the body! Understand this! Flow with this!

Out of the awareness of the body evolves the harmony. Equanimity! And inner balance too!!!

पूर्णमदः पूर्णमिदं पूर्णात पूर्ण मुदच्यते पूर्णष्य पूर्णमादाय पूर्ण मेवा व शिष्यते ॥

[6]

INTELLIGENCE OF THE BODY

Meditation is just to be! Not doing anything!
No action! No thought! No emotions! Just you are!
And it is sheer delight!

MEDITATION: THE WAY TO SELF REALIZATION—2008

Your body is an intelligent mechanism. Your body is always ready to listen to you. But you never talked to it. You have never communicated. You are in the body. You have used the body. But you have never paused to thank the body. It serves you! Not only that, it serves you intelligently as well.

Existence trusts the intelligence of your body. It is more intelligent than you are. All the important functions of the body are given to your body not you. The breathing! The heart beat! The blood circulation! And the digestion! All are given to your body. Wisely enough the existence did not leave these functions with you.

You could have forgotten to breathe like you forget many things. And everything would have been in a mess. You fight with someone and breathing may cease. Sleeping at night you may forget heart beat. And then . . . !

Do you know how much work your digestive system is doing? You go on swallowing things and think that you are doing something great.

The entire digestive system is a miracle. Scientists say if each one of us had to do everything that your digestive system does you would need a huge factory to convert food into blood and other essential elements. And then another system to send these elements to the respective places in desired quantity. A few elements are needed in the brain. And these have to be sent through the bloodstream to the brain.

Others are needed in the eyes, ears, bones or the skin. And body does this meticulously. Not only once or twice! It does this each time you eat and for the entire life! It does not fail. It fails only because of you. It gives you total freedom to bring anything that you wish to bring for digestion. So your body is not to be blamed if the problem arises.

Such intelligence is impeccable.

Have you heard of the alchemists who tried to transform base metals into gold? Your body is far better. It transforms all kinds of crap that you bring into your blood and bones. And not only that, it turns trash into nourishment for brain.

Out of your ice-creams and colas it makes your brain as capable as that of an Albert Einstein, a Rutherford, a Buddha, or a Lau Tzu.

Your brain is such an infinitesimal thing enclosed in skull. However a single brain is capable to contain all the libraries of the world. Its capacity is almost infinite.

Although science is so advanced yet still it cannot convert ice-cream into blood. Perhaps science can never do. And even if it succeeds it will be through brain. Then it will be the miracle of the brain.

Such is the intelligence and the wisdom of the body. This you need to know so that you can create inner balance between body and the mind.

This is the miracle and you go on running behind some petty tricks as miracles. Ummm . . .

[7]

COMMUNION WITH THE BODY

Life surrounds as a musical symphony all around.

MEDITATION: THE ULTIMATE IN HEALING

Communion with the body requires a different wisdom. Once you start communicating with your body things become very easy. You need not force the body for this communion. However it can be persuaded. Do not fight with the body. Your body and its mechanisms are the gift from the God. This is the outcome of Ultimate wisdom. So this cannot be wrong.

Any aggression, violence, and conflict will create tension. Be not in conflict. Be at ease. Let comfort be the criterion. And your body is such a unique gift from God that to fight is not only ugly, instead it will mean denying God.

Your body is the shrine of God. Or the temple of God! God dwells in the body as invisible—formless. God is enshrined in the body as Being. You exist in the body. By the word 'You' I do not mean the false identity—'Ego'. To me 'you' refers to the formless—the being. It is therefore your responsibility to take care of this 'you' enshrined in you.

In the beginning as I am speaking, you may find this absurd. You have never been taught to communicate to your own body. However miracle can happen once you learn the art of communication with your body. Miracles are already happening. But you know not. When I speak my hands move in a gesture. Through speaking it is my mind that is speaking. But the follows the mind! The body is en rapport with the mind.

When you raise your hand you have nothing to do. You simply raise it. Just the very idea that you want to raise it, is enough. The body follows. It is a miracle. No biology! And no psychology has been able to explain this. Because an idea is just an idea! How an idea does transform into a physical message to your hand? Also this does not take any length of time. Just a split of a second and the message is communicated. And sometimes without any time gap the message is communicated.

It appears body runs parallel to the mind. This is very delicate. Learn the art communicating to your body. Many things will happen then. Listen to your body!!!

[8]

LISTENING TO THE BODY IS BENEDICTION!

Life is a song, a dance, and a melody! Flow with its symphony!
A new meaning will arise each finite moment!

ESSENCE OF SUFISM—TAOSHOBUDDHA

Listen to your body. This is benediction. Follow the body. But never try to dominate the body. Once you have started understanding your body 99 percent of your miseries will vanish.

Human body is frozen like ice. And mind is fluid like water. Ice has limitation. Water flows beyond boundaries. Yet still water has its limitations. You can mould mind the way you want. This cannot be done with human body. Body is gross. The body cannot change. You can condition the mind of the child. But you cannot condition or change the body. You can change the fluidity of the mind. There is no way to do this with the body. That will remain connected to its origin. As far as the mind it concerned it can become a Hindu or a Muslim, or a Christian. Such is the freedom of the mind. You have to understand this fluidity of the mind to create balance between body and the mind.

You never listen to the body. At least up to now! Body says 'Stop! Do not eat'! But you listen to the mind. Mind says 'It is very tasty! Really delicious! A little more pleaseee . . .' You do not listen to the body. Body is feeling nauseous. Stomach wants to stop! But not the mind! Mind looks at the taste—the senses. You go on listening to the mind.

If you listen to the body 99 percent of your problems will simply disappear. And the remaining 1% is just accidents, not really problems.

However from the childhood you have been distracted from the body. You are cut off from the body and its mechanism.

The child is crying. Because the child is hungry! But the mother is looking at the clock. The doctor has recommended feed every three hours. The mother is not looking at the child and his indicators. The child is not mind. The child is responding to the body mechanism. And the mother to the 'mind mechanism'! The child is the real clock to look at. She listens to the doctor. The child is hungry. And cries for food! The child needs food now. But you have distracted him from the food. Instead of food you give the child the pacifier.

What can you call this? This is cheating or deceiving. You are giving something false and plastic like. This is destroying the child's natural sensitivity to his body.

From the childhood we do not allow the wisdom of the body. The child cries for the feed. And then crying he goes to sleep. Now the child is fast asleep. His body is sleeping. But you wake the child. Your clock says it is feed time. Again you disturb the body rhythm. Slowly and slowly you disturb the entire being. And a moment comes when the child looses the entire body mechanism and track.

This is how you are allowed to grow. A time comes when you do not know what your body wants. You do not know what your body wants, whether to eat or not. Everything is manipulated by something from outside.

Life goes on like this. Therefore listen to the body!

[9]

BODY IS THE MIRACLE

There is a commune, a synergistic harmony, a rhythm between you and the existence. Only such love can sanctify your being.

ESSENCE OF SUFISM—TAOSHOBUDDHA

Your body is the miracle. It is complex. There is nothing really complex and as subtle as the body. Nothing about this you really know. Your contact with the body is that of the mirror. All you have looked at your body is in the mirror. You have never looked at your body from within.

Your body is the entire universe within.

This is what the mystics have been saying. Your body is micro-cosmos. You look at it from outside. The mystic looks at it from within. The body is so vast within. Millions of the cells are there. Each cell pulsates with its own life. Also each cell functions intelligently. Something that seems almost incredible, impossible and unbelievable!

Each day you eat food. And body transforms the food into blood, bones, marrow etc. You eat food, and the body transforms it into consciousness, and thought. Each moment a miracle happens. And each cell functions systematically. There is an inner order and discipline. This seems almost impossible. Seventy million cells are there in one single body.

Each cell has its own soul. And see how well it functions. These cells work in a coherence, rhythm and harmony. And one thing more! The same cells become the eyes, the skin, liver, heart and so on. These cells specialize to become specialized ones. The entire movement is silent, subtle, and rhythmic.

Go into this mystery. Remember you are rooted in this mystery. The body is your earth. And you are rooted in the earth.

Your consciousness is like the tree in the body. Your thoughts are the fruits that grow on the tree. And your meditations are the flowers that blossom on this tree. Still you are rooted in the body. The body supports it. Your body supports everything that you are doing.

You love! The body supports it. When you hate body supports it. You want to kill someone! The body supports you as well. In compassion, love, hate, anger, in every possible way body supports you.

You are rooted in the body. You are nourished in the body. Even in your realization your body supports you.

Body is your friend. It is not the enemy. Listen to its language. Decode the language. And by and by as you enter the book of body and you start turning its pages you will become aware of the whole mystery of life.

In condensed form it is in your body. Magnified a million times it is spread all over the world. And the entire cosmos too!

[10]

UNFOLD THE MYSTERIES!

The day you accept total responsibility for all that is happening in your life will begin the process of transformation.

MEDITATION: THE ULTIMATE IN HEALING—TAOSHOBUDDHA

Your body has all the mysteries. All the mysteries of the cosmos are condensed in your body. Your body is mini cosmos. The difference between the cosmos and the body is that of quantity alone. Just a single atom contains in its womb the entire secret of the matter. The body contains the secrets of the cosmos. You need not go outwards to discover these secrets. Go inwards!

For this your body has to be taken care of. Never be against your body. Also never condemn it. By condemning your body you are condemning God indirectly. Because in the deepest core or the recess of your body dwells God. God has chosen you body as His abode. Therein He dwells as Soul. Therefore love your body. Respect it! And take care of it.

Body is simply the vehicle. It can take you to the heaven or the hell. It is neutral. It will take you wherever you want to take it to. Your body is an immensely complex mechanism. Full of beauty, order and awe! Understanding the body you are filled with awe. Then what can be said of the entire cosmos! Because this body is full of so many miracles that I call this as the 'Temple of the divine'!

As your attitude towards the body changes it becomes easy for you to go within. With the change in your attitude your body becomes open to you. It allows you to come in. And as you enter it rejoices. And starts unfolding its myriad mysteries! This is how the secrets of Yoga were known. This is how Lau Tzu unfolded the secrets of 'Tao' that which is.

Yoga did not arise by dissecting dead bodies. Modern science is based on the dissection of dead bodies. There is something basically wrong with this. Modern medicine has not yet been able to know a living body.

To dissect a dead body is one thing. And to know something about it is another thing. However to know something about a living body is a totally different phenomena. There is no way for the modern medicine to know anything about a living body. The only way it comes to know is butcher it. Or cut it open! And the moment you cut it open it is no longer the same! To understand a flower on the stem of a tree is one thing. Its quality is different. And when you cut it to know it is a different phenomenon.

Albert Einstein the man has certain qualities that his corpse cannot have. A poet dies! The body is there! But where is the poetry? There is no difference between the body of an idiot and a genius. You cannot differentiate between the body of a mystic and someone who is not even aware of mysticism. The corpse that modern medicine is like the cage that you are studying and the bird has flown. But still the body contains the divine in it.

I teach you the way to go within consciously. And then study the body from within. I teach you how to watch your body from there. There is tremendous joy in it. It is benediction to see the functioning, and the ticking of life energy through various channels. This is the greatest miracle that has happened in the universe. With awareness you can live through this miracle and then something will happen within you whose aura will manifest in the outer dimension.

SECTION 2

MIND MEDITATIONS

[11]

BODY MIND CONNECTIONS!

And when you blame others for miserable life then transformation cannot happen. And you are moving far away from your innerness.

Almost all problems are psychosomatic. Because body and the mind are inseparable! These cannot be separated. Your mind is the inner part of the body. The invisible one! You can start from the body and reach the mind. Or you can start from the mind and reach the body. There is no division. And what appears to be the watertight compartment like is not so.

Each problem has two shores or edges. These can be tackled through the mind or through the body. And up to now this alone has been the approach. A few believed that all problems are of the body. These are physiologists, the Pavlovians, and the behaviorists. They treat the body. And of course they succeed nearly 50 percent. And they hope that as science grows they will be succeeding more. However they will not succeed beyond 50 percent.

Then there are those who think that all problems evolve from the mind. This is as wrong as the first one. Christian Scientists hypnotists and mesmerists all think that problems are mental. So do psychotherapists. And they too succeed in 50 percent of the cases alone. Beyond this nothing can be done. This is the limit.

Mystical and my own understanding is that each problem has to be understood in its totality. Each problem has to be handled from both sides. Only then man can be cured totally or 100 percent. And whenever science becomes total it will work both ways.

Begin with the body. Body is gross. It is the portal of the mind. Body is the porch of the mind. And because body is gross it can be easily manipulated. For this body has to be freed of all its accumulated structures consciously. And at the same time your mind has to be inspired to move upwards. So that in the process it can start dropping all that has been accumulated. As the accumulated karmas are dropped from the tree of consciousness mind attains to the realm of 'No mind'.

No mind is the beginning of a totally new journey of awakening.

BODY AND MIND ARE INSEPARABLE!

Meditation springs from unknown realm. And when its energy overwhelms you change begins to happen. All that then happens is sublime and divine in nature!

Body and mind are inseparable. Forget it not ever. There are no terms like 'Physiological process' or 'Mental processes. Whatever you do physiologically affects the mind. And whatsoever you do psychologically affects the body. They are not two. Instead they are one.

You take alcohol or drugs physically. This affects the mind. Anger, hate, love etc happens through the mind and it affects the physical or bodily gestures. Such is the inseparable nature of body and mind. It is better to use the word 'body-mind'.

You can say that the body is a solid state of the same energy. And the mind is the liquid state of the same energy. You may be doing something physiologically. This is not just physiological. How is this going to help you in any transformation at mental level? Never wonder! Alcohol or LSD is taken orally but affects the mind.

Also you go on a fast! The fasting is done at the body level. But something happens to the mind. Or from the other end! If you think of sexual thoughts something happens to the body. Your body responds immediately. You think of sex objects! The body prepares immediately.

In Japan children are taught a very simple method to manage anger. Accordingly when you are gripped by anger these children are to do nothing except taking deep breaths. You try this and then you will not be angry any more. When you take deep breath the anger becomes impossible. There are two reasons. You start taking deep breath. However anger requires an altogether different breathing pattern. And without such breathing pattern anger is impossible. For anger to work chaotic breathing is needed.

So when you start taking deep breath anger becomes impossible. When you take consciously deep breath your mind shifts from anger to breathing. Just deep breathing and anger is no more.

With this your mind shifts. When you feel angry and you start taking deep breaths your mind shifts from anger to breathing. And body is in no state to be angry. This is the reason the Japanese are the most disciplined persons on earth.

Such an incident is difficult to find anywhere in the world. This is the routine. However this is happening less and less now. Japan is becoming more and more westernized. In this the traditional values are being lost.

Once while I was in Kyoto I saw a man was hit by a car. He fell down. Quickly got up and thanked the driver before leaving. This was not understood by someone who was with me.

This is possible in Japan. He must have taken deep breath. Then it is possible. With deep breath you are transformed into a different person. In that state you can even thank the person who has tried to kill you. Such is the understanding of a Buddha.

Physiological and psychological processes are not separate. These are one. You can start from one shore and reach the other.

Only this much for now!

[13]

YOU ARE THE TOTALITY!

Meditation is just to be!
Not doing anything!
No action! No thought!
No emotions!
Just you are! And it is sheer delight!

MEDITATION: THE WAY TO SELF REALIZATION—2008

I n a new world of awareness the doctors who treat the body will be meditators. So when the body is suffering there must be something behind it. Everything is interwoven. Thus you cannot treat a person just by treating his body. Real treatment can happen only when you look into his totality. To look into his totality you have to look into your own totality.

Each physician need to learn meditation. Otherwise he can never be a real physician. He may have degrees and license to practice medicine. But to me he can only be a quack unless he does not understand the totality of the person. The result is that he only treats the symptoms.

Someone may have certain symptoms. These symptoms may indicate a migraine, or sinus. You start treating the symptoms. But you have not looked deep within to discover the cause of the symptoms. Maybe the person is worried, or burdened, or depressed. Maybe the person has shrunken so much inside that it hurts now. Maybe the person is thinking too much and is not relaxed. So you can treat the symptoms. Also you can force the symptoms to disappear through medicines and poisons.

Thus symptoms are suppressed. And then these symptoms appear somewhere else. Because the root cause has not been touched!

In reality symptoms cannot be treated. Instead it is the person who has to be treated. Man is an organic being. It may happen that the disease may be in the feet or the hand but the root cause may be in the head. Sometime the root cause and symptoms may be at different places. This is because the person is one organic being.

Not only are various cells connected to one another instead both body and the mind are connected to one another. First the body is connected to the mind. And the body and the mind—the soma and psyche are connected to a transcendental existence or simply soul.

Only this much for now!

14

WHY DO YOU CHOOSE TO BE UNHAPPY (1)?

When you are one, suddenly you see oneness outside!
This is pure ishness! Know this as meditation!

Perhaps this is most difficult and complex human problem. Perhaps as an individual you do not have the answer to this. This concerns you. Therefore you will have to understand and consider it very deeply. You need to be practical about it. This cannot be handled theoretically. This is how life goes on. And this is how you choose to remain unhappy each finite moment. In each circumstance you choose to be sad, depressed, and miserable. There are definite reasons for this.

The first reason is upbringing. This plays an important role. If you are unhappy, you gain something from it. This is your gain that continues. And when you are happy you lose.

The child learns from the beginning. Whenever he is unhappy, everyone becomes sympathetic towards him. He gains sympathy. Everyone tries to show love towards him. He gains love. He gains attention. Attention works like nourishment for ego. It acts as alcoholic stimulant. It gives you energy. And you feel important.

When everyone is looking at you, you become important. And when no one looks at you feel nobody. People looking at you and caring gives you tremendous energy.

Alone, ego ceases to exist. Ego can only survive in togetherness. The more people pay attention the more ego gets strengthened. When someone is completely forgotten ego cannot exist. And in the process it dissolves. Ego needs society, association, clubs etc. All these societies and clubs exist to give you a feeling of something.

From the beginning the child learns this art of politics. The politics implies: look miserable. This is the only way to gain sympathy. Look ill and you will become important. A sick child becomes dictatorial. Everyone pays attention to him. He rejoices this.

When you are happy nobody pays attention. This is the reason that from the very beginning we choose unhappiness, pessimism and misery. This is one reason.

There is still another thing related to this. Whenever you are happy! Whenever you are blissful! Whenever you feel ecstatic everyone become antagonistic and jealous of you. Jealousy means that everyone is antagonistic. No one is friendly. So you learn not to be ecstatic. Then everyone becomes inimical to you. You are trained not to show your bliss, and not to laugh.

Life continues thus full of misery and despondency.

Think it through as it is your life.

Only this much for now!!!

15

WHY DO YOU CHOOSE TO BE UNHAPPY (2)?

Though meditation begins in mind, it is not real meditation! Begin with the mind! One day certainly you will attain to meditation!

MEDITATION: THE WAY TO SELF REALIZATION—2008

Why do you choose to remain miserable? Looks that misery is your very existence! This is important to understand. Only then you can come out of this situation.

Look at the people when they laugh. Their laughter is very calculative. Your laughter is not the belly laugh of Chinese mystic Hotey. Your laughter is not emanating from the deepest core of your being. You first look at the situation, judge it and then you can laugh. Also you to a particular extent! The extent you can tolerate. The extent that will not be taken amiss! The extent where nobody will become jealous!

Your smile is political. The real laughter has disappeared. Bliss remains an unknown and empty word for you. You are not allowed to remain ecstatic. This is almost impossible. When you are miserable you are considered insane. And when you are ecstatic, and dancing everyone feels you are mad. When you are blissful it is considered that something is wrong with you.

This is society that we have created. Miserable you are okay. Then you fit the social fabric. The whole society is miserable more or less. If you become ecstatic everyone will think you have gone berserk, insane.

Society does not allow ecstasy. Ecstasy is the greatest revolution. I emphasize if people become ecstatic the society will have to undergo change. As such society is it is based on misery.

Happy people cannot be led to war. To a blissful person this is all nonsense. A blissful person cannot be obsessed with money. Such a person will not waste his life just accumulating money. And the money will be available when the person is dead. This is absolute madness. But you cannot see this madness unless you are ecstatic.

Each moment life presents different situations, circumstances and conditions. Certain are acceptable to human understanding while others are not. In all circumstances you choose to be unhappy. And to human understanding this is normal while to a meditator it is not. In all circumstances you choose to be unhappy. And slowly and slowly this becomes your musculature. And your entire life centers on this unhappiness.

To be happy is your choice and right. To be happy is a conscious choice only you can make. But in all situations you choose to be unhappy. Remember a happy heart is the door to the beyond, or door to the inner, or door to the being. You tend to be happy or unhappy because of the other or the circumstances. No one chooses to be happy for no reason. A happy heart is filled with gratitude towards the WHOLE. To be happy is the greatest blessing. It unfolds a totally new unknown and unknowable realm.

The moment your mind has to choose, it immediately flows towards misery. Misery is to be downhill. And ecstasy is to be uphill. Ecstasy seems very difficult to reach. However, in reality it is not so. In reality ecstasy is downhill and misery is uphill. Misery is very difficult to achieve. But you have it already.

No one wants to be miserable. And yet still everyone is miserable. This much for now!

SECTION 3

THE BODY—
MIND BALANCING!

16

UNDERSTANDING MISERY!

When mind ceases, you are beyond it!
Only then real meditation begins. Know this as your essence!

Misery seems to be downhill and ecstasy seems to be uphill. It seems ecstasy is very difficult to attain. However in reality it is not so! Instead it is quite contrary. Ecstasy is downhill. Misery is uphill. Misery is difficult to attain. But you have to achieve. Misery is against nature. And the irony is that no one wants to be miserable yet still everyone is miserable.

Your society, social values, education, culture, cultural and religious custodians, parents and teachers all have done a great job. The outcome is a breed of miserable creatures. Each child is born ecstatic. Every child is born with the seed of awakening. However in the process of growth somewhere everything goes wrong. And the result is that every one dies as a mad person.

The work of the master is how to regain your childhood. How to make you innocent once again? Once you attain to your childhood innocence there remains no problem. This does not mean there are no moments of misery in the life of a child. Certainly there are moments of misery. Yet still there is no misery. This you have to understand.

Certainly a child can become miserable. He can be unhappy. Intensely unhappy in a moment! There is awe, and wonder in his life too. However in the moments of unhappiness he is totally with unhappiness that there is division. You separate the child from unhappiness he ceases to exist. His unhappiness is not separate. He is utterly involved in his unhappiness. So when you become one with unhappiness, it is no more unhappiness. If you become one with it, it has beauty of its own.

Look at a child who is spoilt. If he is angry, then his entire energy becomes anger. Nothing is left behind. He reserves nothing. He has moved and become anger. No one manipulates his anger. There is no mind. The child has become anger. But he is not angry. Only then you can see the beauty—the flowering of anger. The child never looks ugly. Even in his anger he looks beautiful. He looks more intense, vital and like a volcano ready to explode. Such a small child! Full of tremendous energy! Such an atomic being! Ready to explode the entire universe!

After the anger has subsided the child will be utterly silent. Relaxed! You may think it is miserable to be in such anger. However such is not the case with the child. He has enjoyed every moment of this.

When you are one with it! You are total with anything you are blissful. And when you are separate from anything even if it be happiness you will remain miserable.

This is the key. To be separate you are like an island of ego. Then misery is the outcome. To be one! To be so intensely! To be flowing with whatever the stream of life brings, you are no more. And when you are no more life is blissful or benediction.

The choice is always yours. In the process of life you have always chosen the wrong. This has become your habit. Then there is no choice left for you.

Be alert and awake. Each moment when you are choosing to be miserable remember it is your choice. It is your life. Only you can blossom into a beautiful flower. Even this mindfulness will certainly help. And the 'alertness' that this is my choice, my responsibility will not only be helpful instead you will feel the difference. With this alertness the quality of the mind will change. Then it will be easier for you to move towards happiness.

Once you know this is your choice then everything becomes a game. Then even if you love to be miserable, be miserable. The only thing you have to remember is that this is your choice. Nobody is responsible. This is your stage show. If you like this miserable way! If you want to pass the stream of your life through misery, then this is your choice. You are playing this. But play it well with totality.

Never ask people how not to be miserable. This is absurd. Also never ask masters how to be happy. There are people who will fool you. First you create misery and then you ask how to uncreate it. You go on creating misery because you are unaware.

You know not what you chose. Be alert. From now on try to be happy and blissful.

[17]

UNDERSTANDING ANGER

Anger is the outcome of ego and sex! Both sex and ego are the functions of the mind and lack of understanding this leads to the spate of anger!! Without ignorance ego ceases to exist! And without ego ignorance and anger has no value no use!

SONG ETERNAL-BHAGWAD GITA AN ENCHANTING IMPOSSIBILITY—TAOSHOBUDDHA

In the process of inward journey understanding anger is essential. Anger cannot be managed. In doing so anger goes deep in the subconscious layer! There it is nourished and nurtured. Suppressed by social norms, cultural values and traditions anger gains strength and momentum!

Unwanted it expresses itself even when the circumstance does not call far. Thus in the process of its evolution anger goes on gaining momentum. And explodes like a force. And when anger gains momentum it brings with it fear, ignorance and violence.

Fear is the outcome of ignorance. Ignorance is the ornament of ego. Together these nourish and nurture anger. Without ignorance ego ceases to exist. And without ego ignorance and anger has no value no use. Remember when light of awareness and understanding descends ignorance disappears in the oblivion. And thus vanishes the ego too.

Thereafter what remains is the light of truth. Anger dissolves in that light.

However in the absence, despondency and agitation breeds in human mind! Filled with negativities life full of anger goes on unabated.

Because of unfulfilled desires, lack of understanding of sex energy and its transcendence a process breeds in human mind. Anger is the outcome of this. And you continue to drown in the valley of darkness.

Anger is the downward movement of existential bio energy. When this bio energy manifests through the lower psycho centers it breeds negativities. Without clearing such negativities journey to higher reams is impossible. This existential bio energy is given to you to first understand its purpose. Understand the techniques to allow the upward journey. In the process of upward movement light descends. You attain not only fulfillment through sex you transcend it as well.

One day you come into life through the functioning of this energy through the sex center. And through this center as well you transcend beyond sex one day. You attain inner harmony at physical, emotional, and intellectual level. What a benediction?

Without such an understanding and balance between the physical, emotional, and intellectual level harmony does not happen. And without harmony within emotions play a devil's role. And to such a being is always denied harmony's peaceful existence.

Anger can be managed somehow. Management of anger is impossible without suppression. And anything suppressed gains strength. Becomes a force impossible to reckon with!

The first criterion is to understand this. And in that understanding itself the process of its dissolution begins.

A conscious catharsis is the sure way to dissolve anger. Many techniques are there for catharsis. However this is an individual process. There are generalized techniques. However individualized techniques are more effective. These are designed to suit the individual needs. Master penetrates your unconscious and sub-conscious layers and designs the technique suitable to your growth and thus sets the process of transformation.

Allow an understanding to dawn in you. The process of dissolution of anger will certainly begin. Understand anger! Allow it to dissolve!! Only this much for now!!

[NOTE: SEE SECTION 3 'MEDITATION TECHNIQUES' AND PAGE 260 OF **MEDITATION: THE WAY TO SELF REALIZATION** BY TAOSHOBUDDHA—A STERLING PAPERBACK 2008

Or send me a mail at www.http//mailtaoshobuddha@gmail.com; Visit Web site: http://dhyan-samadhi.webs.com/staff.htm]

[18]

TWO WAYS TO LIVE

Awakening is the beginning in the journey of transformation!

MEDITATION: THE WAY TO SELF REALIZATION—2008

Remember there are two ways to live. To be! And to know! The two ways are: one is the way of effort, will, ego or struggle. The other is the way of effortlessness, no struggle. This is the path of 'Total let go with the existence.'

Almost all the religions teach you the first. Fight against nature! Fight against world. Fight against your own body. And fight against your own mind. This is the only way to reach truth! The ultimate! The eternal! However this is the way to power! To ego! This has utterly failed. In the long history of human consciousness a few countable ones have achieved the ultimate experience of life through the way of struggle and will. The number is so few that this is exception.

My way is the way of 'Total let go'. Never go against the current of life—the existence. It is not against you. Move with it. Fighting with the river of life will tire and ultimately drown you. And then you can move no more. The river of life is vast and you are infinitesimal.

In this vastness of existence you are even smaller than an atom. Then how can you fight against the whole? This is not only foolish instead unintelligent as well. The existence has created you. Then how can this be against you. Your body is the temple of the unknown. The nature is your mother.

Your body is your life. So it cannot be antagonistic to you. It goes on serving you in spite of your continuous fight with it. It serves you when you are awake and asleep. Who goes on breathing? You are fast asleep and snoring even. Your body has its wisdom. It continues to breath. Heart continues to beat. And body goes on functioning even without you. It functions better in your absence. Your presence always disturbs. Your mind is conditioned by the people who have created antagonism in you against the body.

I teach you to be friendly towards the body. I am not in favor of renouncing the world. The world is yours. Nothing that exists is against you. But you have learned the other way around. Rejoicing not renouncing is the way to transformation. The only question is learning the art to transform poison into nectar.

You will find many medicines with the word 'poison' written on it. However in the hands of a scientific expert the poison becomes life saving medicine. Poison transformed becomes capable of saving life.

When you find that somewhere your body, nature, the world is against you remember one thing always. Certainly it must be your ignorance. Maybe you do not know the art of living. You are unaware that the existence is not against you. You are born out of it. You live in it. It has given you everything. But you are unaware. There is no gratefulness in you. On the contrary all religions have been teaching you to condemn you from the very beginning.

Any religion that teaches you to condemn life is poisonous. It is anti life. It is not in your service. Also it is not in the service of the existence. But why does the question arise?

All the so called religions went against nature. Why this logic is created that unless you are against the world only then transformation can be possible. Why such a division is created between this world and the life beyond? There is a reason for this.

If this world is not to be renounced but lived totally then the priest will not be needed. To renounce this world you have to repress the natural instincts. In such a case you will remain in a sorry state. Being against the nature you can never be healthy. You can never be whole. You will always be split and schizophrenic. In that case you will need someone who can help you. Of course you will need the priest.

It is quite natural when you are guilty you go to the church, mosque, temple or synagogue. You seek the assistance of the priest to help you. In your deep darkness, which is created by them alone you find yourself so helpless. You need protection. You need someone who can guide your steps. You are so desperate that you do not ever think about whether the priest knows anything more than you do or whether he is just a paid servant.

You have never looked within. If you are in misery, in suffering, in anxiety and in anguish you are discontinued with life. You do not see any meaning in life. You are dragging yourself towards death.

The darkness is growing deeper. With each day you are coming closer to death. This is the time to change your being. You do not have much time.

But the religions are teaching you the methods of fighting. But these lead you nowhere. Instead these simply spoil your joys of life. They go on poisoning everything that is enjoyable in life. They have created a sad humanity.

I would like the humanity full of love! Full of song! Full of celebration! And full of dance!

[19]

LIFE IS SONG! A DANCE! A CELEBRATION!

Love is union. Because in a union those who join together remain separate. In a unity they dissolve. They melt into one another. They become one.

THE SECRETS OF BHAKTI—Taoshobuddha
STERLING PAPERBACK—2009

I want to clarify something from the very beginning. I want to clarify that my way is the way of the existence. The way of song! A dance! And a celebration!

Each finite moment there is existential sound or a 'Naad' echoing in the cosmos. In a state of meditation one can not only hear instead the mystics have heard this sound echoing deep within. A Buddha, Nanak, a Lau Tzu, a Jesus, a Mohammed, a Mahabir, and a Marpa have not only heard the echo in the existence instead deep within their being as well.

The rivers, the mountain, the trees, the oceans are in a constant dance, and celebration each moment. Only you have lost the capability of this celebration.

My method implies not to go against the current. To go upstream! This is unwise. You cannot fight because the current of nature is too big and too strong. Try to learn from a dead body. Dead know a certain secret that even the living do not know.

Dead bodies float. And living ones drown. This is very strange because as soon as one dies he surfaces again. Living one goes under the water and drowns. And once drowned one dies and body comes to the surface. Certainly dead knows the secret. One wonders why rivers and ocean behave differently with living and the dead. The dead is in a state of total let go. He is not even swimming. The dead body is not doing anything. It simply floats.

The best swimmer simply floats. The ultimate swimmer or the master swimmer does not even swim. He simply floats. He just moves with the current. Wherever the river leads he is always ready to move. And the river always moves towards the ocean.

Each river leads to the ocean. The river never bothers if it is a holy or unholy river. Holy or unholy each river is moving towards the final merger with the ocean. So are you! You just float with the river of life. It matters not where the river may take you to. The river of life may drift somewhat. However merger with the ocean is the ultimate goal.

This is trust. Trusting in existence that wherever it leads, it always leads to the right path, to the right goal! It is not your enemy.

Trust in nature that wherever it is taking you, there alone is your home. If the whole humanity learns the art of relaxation, or let go instead of fight and struggle there will be a great change in the quality of consciousness. Relaxed person, simply moving silently, in total harmony with the flow of the river, without any goal having no ego is the very essence of the religious one.

In such a state of relaxed floating you cannot have ego. This is meditation. Ego needs effort. Ego is doer. And by floating you become a non-doer. In such a state of non doing or inaction you will be surprised to know that all miseries and anxieties start slipping from your hand.

You are then contented with whatever existence gives you.

Only this much for now!

[20]

TO BE FLOATING IS BENEDICTION!

First, love gives you unity in your innermost core. Then you are no more a body, no more a mind, no more a soul. You are simply one.

THE SECRETS OF BHAKTI—Taoshobuddha
STERLING PAPERBACK—2009

To be floating with existence! To be in harmony with the existence! To be contended with whatever the existence gives you is benediction. And benediction is blissful. This bliss explodes into meditation one day.

I have heard of a Sufi mystic who was travelling. Each evening he would thank the existence looking at the stars. He would say, 'You have done so much for me and I have never been able to repay it and also I will never be able to repay it.' This always baffled his disciples. Some of them even felt disgusted because at times the life was really arduous.

The Sufi was rebellious. It happened that for three days they had no food. The village was full of orthodox Mohammaden. They had joined a rebellious group of Sufis. As a result there was no shelter no food. They had to sleep in the desert. They were thirsty and hungry. It was now the third day. At the end of the third day the Sufi again prayed to thank the existence.

The Sufi, as usual, thanked, 'I am so grateful. You have been doing so much for us. We can never repay this.'

Hearing this one of the disciples got angry and said, 'This is too much. Now for three days we do not have food or shelter. Now tell me what the existence has been doing for us for the last three days. What are you thanking for?'

Hearing this Sufi laughed and said, 'You still seem to be unaware of what the existence has done for us. These three days have been very significant for me. We were hungry, and thirsty. Without shelter! We were rejected, condemned and stoned. I was watching within. There was no anger. I am thanking the existence for this. Its gifts are invaluable. I can never repay. Three days of hunger, thirst, sleeplessness! Yet still I felt no enmity, anger, hatred, or failure. It must be your grace.'

'These three days have revealed so many things to me which would not have been possible if we were given food, shelter and reception. And you are asking what I am thanking existence for? I will thank existence even if I am dying. I will be thankful even for death. Because in death the mysteries go on revealing! Death is not the end. It is the culmination of life. *Death is the Purna Ahuti of the Yagna of life.*'

Learn to flow with existence. Life will unfold a new meaning.

Life will unfold a new meaning. Love now and here.

[21]

LEARN TO FLOW WITH EXISTENCE!

*Love is the way of preparing the soil of your heart. If you are full of love,
the world is full of God. They go parallel.*

THE SECRETS OF BHAKTI—*Taoshobuddha*

A STERLING PAPERBACK-2009

Flow with existence. Life will be a benediction. Do not have guilt or wounds. Never condemn the actions. Actions are like dry leaves that are no more needed on the tree of consciousness. You never condemn the leaves when these turn gold and fall from the tree of consciousness.

So too for soul's journey such actions are no more needed. These must fall from the tree of consciousness.

Therefore never condemn actions of anyone. Actions fall like dry leaves from the tree. Never judge anyone from his actions. Feel the presence of the person. Also feel when the presence is no more. By nature you tend to judge a person by his actions. Not by what he is. You need to understand what actions are. It is the thought that becomes action in the field of objects and beings. Thoughts need to be expressed.

When thoughts are transformed in field of activity actions are born. Actions can be expressed consciously and unconsciously. In most of the cases the actions evolve out of unconsciousness. Evolving out of unconscious is okay. Because unconscious layer is 9 times of your conscious layer! And anything not understood at the conscious level goes in unconscious layer. For transformation the master communicates through your unconscious layer.

Thus when you are in commune of a master knowingly or unknowingly things start emanating from the unconscious layer. Actions are the outcome of such phenomena.

All that is unwanted needs to fall from the tree. When the fruits ripe naturally these fall from the tree! In the process of transformation something like this happens.

Do not fight with your body, or nature or anything else. Learn to flow with existence. Never allow guilt and wounds to inflict you. Be calm, at peace, and collected.

With this you will become more alert, aware, and conscious. This will lead to the ocean of ultimate awakening or Liberation. Thus will continue the process of transformation of human consciousness!

22

BODY IS YOUR FRIEND!

God is the echo from the universe. When you are in love, the echo is there.
When you are not in love, how can there be an echo?

ESSENCE OF SUFISM—Taoshobuddha 2010

B ody is your friend. Consciousness dwells in body. However all the religions have been teaching you antagonism against body? You are taught to fight against nature. All that is natural is condemned. They force you to do something unnatural. Without being against body and all that is natural you cannot get out of the imprisonment of biology, physiology, physiology and all those invisible walls that surround you.

If you are in harmony with the body, mind and heart religions proclaim that you cannot go beyond yourself. Religious custodians have poisoned your being. You live in the body. But you are not allowed to love your body.

Human body serves you for seventy, eighty, ninety or even hundred years. There is no scientific mechanism that can be compared with the mechanism of the body. Its complexities and miracles are unique. You do not have time to pause even for a moment to introspect. Or thank the existence for all that it has given you as the gift of body. You go on treating body as enemy. But body is your friend.

Body takes care of you in every possible way. It takes care of you even when you are awake and asleep. Imagine you are asleep and a spider crawls on your leg. The leg throws off the spider without bothering you. It has a small brain of its own. And for such small matters it need not go to the central system. So too when you are sleeping and mosquito bites you, your hand moves to move it or kill it. Your sleep is not disturbed. So while you sleep the body goes on protecting you. It does certain things that you are not even aware of it.

The hand is not supposed to have brain. However certainly it has a small brain of its own. Definitely each cell of the body has its own intelligence and small brain. There are millions of cells in the body. Also there are millions of small brains. Thus body takes care of you.

You are not even aware of this. You have never paid attention to the mechanism and intelligence of the body. Introspect and meditate over the functions of the body.

23

UNDERSTANDING YOUR BODY!

God is an echo that lingers in your heart like the dissolving notes of a melody that you have once heard in the wilderness.

ESSENCE OF SUFISM-Taoshobuddha
STERLING PAPERBACK-2010

You have never respected your body. And without respect understanding will not dawn. Understanding your body and its mechanism will lead you to freedom one day.

Have you ever noticed that you go on eating all kinds of things? And you never bother what will happen when you swallow these foods. You never ask your body or its inner mechanism or its chemistry will it be able to digest all that you are swallowing. Somehow your inner mechanism goes on functioning for almost a century. Automatically it replaces parts that have worn out. It expels all defective parts. And you have nothing to do for this. Creates new parts! It happens on its own. The body has certain mechanism and wisdom of its own.

All the religions say, 'You have to fight always. You have to move against the current.' You are not to listen to your body. And do just the opposite to what the body asks you to do. You completely forget that body serves you without any payment, or salary or any other reward.

This fight against body gives you tremendous ego power. When body seeks food and you deny your ego is strengthened. 'No' has great power. You are the master. You reduce the body to a mere slave. You force your body to keep its mouth shut. Whatever ego decides goes on.

Never fight with the body. It is your friend. It is nature's gift to you. In every way you are connected to the existence. You are connected to breathing. To sunrays! To flowers! And to moon light! You are the part of the whole. You are whole. Yet still it has given you individuality. This is the miracle of the existence.

You are the part of existence. It has made everything possible for you. More than this it has given you individuality.

24

BODY IS BENEDICTION!

It is only you who are reflected again and again in millions of ways.
It is you who are thrown back to yourself again and again.
If you are in love, God is.

Essence of Sufism—*A STERLING PAPAERBACK 2010*

Being is harmony with body creates inner harmony. Inner harmony leads to outer harmony. And together inner and outer harmony brings equanimity.

Instead of going against the current, flow with the current! Be in a total let go. Allow life to take its own course. Do not force anything on the body. Not even for the sake of any holy book! Or any holy ideal! Never disturb your harmony!

Nothing is more significant than to be harmonious. Harmony is bliss.

Respect life. There is nothing holier than life. To be holy is divine. Life is precious in small things. But all the religions teach you big things. The strategy is clear. You are asked to do big things so that your name is remembered afterwards. All this appeals to your ego!

There is nothing big or small. This is the approach of the Mind. Life consists of small things. Life is meaningful in small things. If you are interested in big things meaning will disappear from life.

Life is meaningful in sipping a cup of tea. Going for a walk! But going nowhere in particular! Just for a walk! No goal! No end! Cooking food for someone you love! Cooking food for you! Washing clothes! Cleaning the floor! Watering the garden! Such very small things make life meaningful. Saying hello to a stranger, which is not needed, as there is no business in it, is indeed meaningful. Then you can say hello to a tree or a flower or sing a song with the birds.

Birds go on singing each morning and you do not feel any oneness with the birds. Return the call of the birds. Just small things! And nothing else you will discover meaningful in life.

Sometimes be with the flower! Just sitting by the side! Doing nothing! Just being one with the flower! No thought! No actions! No feelings! Just sitting by the side of the flower something will happen. So too sit at the sea shore. Feel the waves arising deep within you. Feel the sound of the roaring of the ocean echo deep within you. A new meaning will arise. And this meaning will connect you to your being. And out of that will spring forth your essential nature.

This is inner healing! This is Meditativeness! This is Beingness. This is meditation the ultimate in healing!

Meditation is ultimate in healing!

SECTION 4

MEDITATION THE ULTIMATE IN HEALING!

25

'CHOOSE TO BE HAPPY'!

'Always Choose To Be Happy'

NAQSHBANDI SUFI SHAKUNTALA DEVI
ESSENCE OF SUFISM-Taoshobuddha

ALWAYS CHOOSE TO BE HAPPY' is the very essence of finite existence overflows the essence of **Naqshbandi Sufi Shakuntala Devi.**

Keep your eyes slightly closed. Make yourself comfortable. It matters not what posture you choose. Choose the one that makes you comfortable. Only then you can move from the realm of the body and the mind to the realm of the being.

Allow the music to sink deep within you. This is not merely music or the words. Through this flows the energy field of the master. Feel it deep within you as I take you on this eternal voyage.

Each moment life presents different situations, circumstances and conditions. Certain are acceptable to human understanding while others are not.

In all circumstances you choose to be unhappy. And to human understanding this is normal while to a meditator it is not. In all circumstances you choose to be unhappy. This is not your essential nature. And slowly and slowly this becomes your musculature. And your entire life centers on this unhappiness.

Be aware of this situation. Awake and arise! Therefore o Friend this is your right to 'Choose to be happy!'

I teach you to be happy under all circumstances. Be it sorrow or pain or anything else always 'Choose to be happy'! Life will begin to move in a new dimension.

You will find this difficult in the beginning. I am here to bring an energy field that will help you make this beginning. And once you have consciously decided for this journey will begin.

How long will you continue the saga of misery and unhappiness? Now is the time!

To be happy is your choice and right. To be happy is a conscious choice only you can make. But in all situations you choose to be unhappy.

Remember a happy heart is the door to the beyond, or door to the inner, or door to the being. You tend to be happy or unhappy because of the other or the circumstances.

No one chooses to be happy for no reason. A happy heart is filled with gratitude towards the WHOLE. To be happy is the greatest blessing. It unfolds a totally new unknown and unknowable realm.

One Sufi Naqshbandi master Shakuntala Devi, always used to bless any one bowing to her by saying **"BE ALWAYS HAPPY"**. If you really decipher these simple words, these will manifest a totally new realm.

When a master says something, the seeker needs to introspect on these words. The master can never be wrong or unconscious. The very fact that he or she is a master implies now something has changed within.

A master may look like you, but in reality he differs in his understanding of the cosmic phenomena and awareness. None of his actions are ever guided by unconscious. Even when he moves his hands he is totally aware of this.

Let this be your meditation each moment. A new meaning will unfold in life. Serenity, blessedness will engulf you. Only then it can be said that you are living in the image of a master. Then something of the master, his awareness, his understanding, will be part of you as blessing.

Awake and arise O mortal being! Immortality pulsates within you. Allow it to overflow. The overflow needs the door. A 'Happy Heart', a 'Heart full of Gratitude' is the door. And 'Choose to be happy' is the window. Through this window look at the existence each finite moment!

A new meaning will arise.

[26]

MEDITATION—'EK ONKAR SATNAM...'

*Ek-onkār saṯ nām karṯā purakẖ nirbẖa-o nirvair akāl mūraṯ
ajūnī saibẖa'n guru parsāḏ!*

JAPJI SAHIB—SONGS OF NANAK

This is the *Mool mantra*. It has two parts. The Invocation and the Explanation of the attributes!

Begin the message with invocation. **'Ek Onkar Satnam'** is the Invocation. Flow with the melody and the sound as it continues like an undercurrent. Feel this sound within.

This is the essence. This is the meditation. The entire message and the Sikh religion are condensed in these three words. After this all that Nanak spoke is the explanation.

Bolo Sri Vahi Guru . . .

Now that you have spoken this now feel the energy overflowing from the master towards you like an invisible current. Only an enchanted heart can feel this deep within.

Keep your eyes closed! Remain in a comfortable position.

'Ek Onkar Satnam' is the essence of JAP JI. This is the first offering of Nanak to humanity. After this communion with his beloved JAP JI IS THE FIRST WORDS THAT EVOLVED OUT OF NANAK!

JAP JI IS THE ECSTASY OF NANAK! NOTHING IS MORE SUBLIME IN THE MESSAGE OF NANAK THAN JAP JI! JAP JI IS THE BEING OF NANAK! HIS FRAGRANCE!

JAP JI is such an offering of NANAK.

Never consider this story of Nanak disappearing in the river or drowning and then appearing in front of God literally. If you think so then you are still an infant—juvenile. You have only grown physically. Consciousness or wisdom is not yet born in you.

What to do? Something sublime has to be communicated. Language is the only medium. This is the problem with the masters. They have to choose the words from the language. Words and language has its limitations.

All that Nanak wants to communicate is magnanimous. Beyond words! And cannot be put into words! Words are incapable to manifest its magnanimity. So this remains the barrier.

Allow this to sink in you. The entire creation will become godly. In that inner harmony and oneness everything and everyone dances in that glory.

Ek onkār sat nām!

The day your inner vision opens, you will realize only that energy field surrounds you.

He is one! His very form is **Onkar**! The existential! He is **Satnam**! Embodiment of truth! Truth incarnate!

The cosmic doer! Beyond fear! Beyond prejudice! Beyond time and space is his sublime existence!

Born out of his own free will he ever remains unborn! Yet still he is the cause of his own existence! Such are his attributes Sacred and Sublime!

How can one attain to this presence!!

Certainly not by your own efforts alone! Be assured! By the grace of the Master! Let this be your trust and certitude as well!!!

Ek onkār sat nām!

SANGAT BOLO SRI VAHE GURU . . . VAHE GURU . . . VAHE GURU JI KA KHALSA VAHE GURU JI KI FATEH . . .

Onkar is the only existential sound. It was in the beginning of the creation. It will be in the dissolution of creation. Also it is now here! You will feel it deep within as the noise of the mind dissolves!

Nanak says that which is cannot be given any name. All names are given by man. Onkar is the only name that is not given by any one. Ram, Krishna, Allah are all names given by men of different sects. The only name that is not created is Onkar.

And why this name Onkar?

You are a constant chatterbox. Thought keeps on floating on the inner sky. Constantly waves appear on the surface. When thoughts are no more! Waves have subsided and merged in the ocean, and you drown in your innerness, only then you can hear a mystical sound.

Ek onkār sat nām!

This sound is uncreated. No one has created it. This is the sound of the existence. This is the echo of the existence. Onkar is the way of existence. This name is not assigned by anyone. Aum is not a word. This is the sound. Not only an ordinary sound, is it unique as well. Without any source, uncreated this remains hidden in the existence itself.

Drown in the serenity that is happening around you.

All sounds are created by friction. A musician vibrates the strings of the instrument and thus creates a sound. This sound is created because of the friction between the strings and the finger.

The river flows. A sound arises through the flow. This is the sound created when water strikes the shore. You sit by the waterfall. There is a sound. Water falls on the rock a sound is created. This is the sound of the waterfall. Breeze blows and rustling it passes through the leaves. Rustling is the sound created between the breeze and the tree leaves.

We speak! Singer sings! Meditator chants! All such sounds are created because of duality. When all duality vanishes a sound continues as echo. This is the sound of Aum. Remember Aum is not a word. Each language be it, Hindi, Sanskrit or Gurumukhi has a special letter to represent this sound.

Nanak says this is Onkar! This is the only authentic name of that which is. Nanak calls this NAAM. Again and again Nanak uses this word NAAM.

As you attain to silence meditativeness happens Ram transforms into 'Onkār.' Such is the experience of all the mystics: one may begin with any name ultimately everything dissolves into 'Onkar.'

Allow the silence of Onkar to deepen in you.
As silence descends 'onkār' is. 'Onkār' is always only you need to attain to silence. Nanak sings:

'Ek-onkār Sat nām'!

OM is the sound when everything else disappears from your being! No thoughts! No dreams! No projections! No expectations! Not even a single ripple!

Your whole lake of consciousness is simply there! Silent too! It has become just a mirror. In those rare moments you hear the sound of silence. It is the most valuable experience because not only it shows a quality of the inner music instead it shows that the inner being is harmony, joy, and blissfulness. All this is implied in the silent music of OM Nanak says.

You begin with labial sound. As this continues a moment comes when you are not saying it. Then even with saying you will miss the real thing. You have to hear it! You have to be utterly calm and quiet! And then suddenly it is all around you like a very subtle dance. Or like a subtle melody. And the moment you are able to hear it, you have entered into the very secrets of existence. You have become so subtle that now you deserve all the mysteries to be revealed to you. Existence waits till you are ready. Matters not how low it has to wait!

This silence is not created by the musician. The musician is creating the sounds and leaving the gaps as a contrast, so that you can experience something of what happens to the mystic in his inner world.

Meditation gives you this feeling, for the first time. This is your authentic reality. This is existential. This is the pulse. This is being. This is OM. This is 'Ek-Onkār'. This is the EXISTENTIAL ONENESS that Nanak calls 'Ek-Onkār.'

EK Onkar SATNAM!

Feel it within. You go on drowning in the vastness of this existential sound.

Life will unfold inner treasures.

MEDITATION—
'HUKUM RAJAI CHALNA . . .'

'HUKUM rajai chalna Nanak likhiya naal'

JAPJI SAHIB—SONGS OF NANAK

HUKUM rajai chalna Nanak likhiya naal' is the essence of man's inner or eternal existence. Such is the message of a master, a flower of the existence Nanak.

Feel it deep within. Such are not ordinary words. And not spoken by a mortal being. Through these words the very essence, the consciousness, the being of Nanak pulsates.

Allow the essence of these words enter deep within you. Like an intoxicating elixir these will begin the process of transformation deep within.

Allow an understanding of this eternal message of Nanak evolve from deep within. Life will move in a new dimension. A dimensionless dimension of eternity!

Now let me take you on an inner journey to the realm of the master—Nanak.

Keep your eyes slightly closed. Make yourself comfortable. It matters not what posture you choose. Choose the one that makes you comfortable. Only then you can move from the realm of the body and the mind to the realm of the being.

Allow the music to sink deep within you. This is not merely music or the words. Through this flows the energy field of the master. Feel it deep within you as I take you on this eternal voyage.

There is a synergistic harmony in the existence. Everything moves in harmony. No one is doing anything and yet still everything moves without a mistake. Know this as cosmic law. Because of this harmony we call existence as 'COSMOS'. And the law that allows the things to happen is called 'The Cosmic Law'. Nanak calls this harmony as 'Hukum'. Whatever you call this the essence and the understanding of the masters remains the same.

Feel this harmony deep within first. The body, the mind, and the intellect are dissolving into oneness. First feel this oneness within. And then it will create an energy field in the outer world of beings and objects.

Such is the essence of the master—Nanak.

You cannot see beyond finiteness. Time is not linear. This is the reason that you do not agree with all that is happening in and around you.

Never think the existence to be unwise. When the leaves fall from the tree during autumn there is a reason. When new leaves begin to sprout during spring there is a meaning. The existence is wiser than the entire wisdom of the human beings.

HUKUM RAJAI CHALNA NANAK LIKHIYA NAAL!

Feel the energy that this composition creates within.

Understand the very essence of it! Only then you can feel it! With feeling flowing will happen on its own! And then the spring of your life is not far! Your life will certainly become a 'Valley of Flowers!'
Flow with life! Each circumstance and situation will begin to shower myriad flowers each finite moment.
HUKUM RAJAI CHALNA NANAK LIKHIYA NAAL!

Allow these words, the essence, and the melody to linger in your being like the dissolving notes of a sweet melody.

A new meaning will arise!

[28]

'SABHANA JIYA KA EK DATA . . .'

'SABHANA JIYA KA EK DATA SO MAIN BISUR NA JAIE'!

JAPJI SAHIB—SONGS OF NANAK

He alone is the life—giver, the sustainer of the entire existence! No one else indeed! This is the Mantra! This is Ultimate Understanding! This I may never ever forget even for a moment!

An ecstatic Nanak sings:

'SABHANA JIYA KA EK DATA SO MAIN BISUR NA JAIE'!

Mystically Nanak reminds you each finite moment:

'This I may never ever forget'! Both knowingly and unknowingly! In waking, dreaming, or deep sleep state! In conscious or unconscious of awareness!

Feel the energy field of Nanak overflowing through these words.

He alone is the master of all beings! And this I may never ever forget even for a moment!

Nanak is not saying to remember this. Instead he is reminding you not to forget this any moment.

Try to understand this.

When something is imposed from outside you will have to make efforts to remember this. And in trying to remember you may forget again and again. This is effort. Not spontaneous!

'SABHANA JIYA KA EK DATA SO MAIN BISUR NA JAIE'!

Introspect, not the words! Instead the essence of the message of Nanak!

Feel the soul of these words 'SO MAIN BISUR NA JAIE'!

When these words grow deep within and spring from the deepest core of your being you need not remember. Then you can never forget even for a moment.

Then you need not make any effort to remember this. Instead out of inner joy and ecstasy you will say:

'SO MAIN BISUR NA JAIE'!

This I may never forget! Forget even for a moment!

How can this happen?

Look at a pregnant woman. A change has taken place within her biology. The change has happened at the gross level.

As a result something has begun to grow deep within. A new life now pulsates deep within. Her each action is now guided by this awareness. This awareness that she is carrying a new life within is not imposed from outside. Had it been so then she may forget at times. This does not happen at all.

Such is awareness. Awareness of a growth! Awareness of a new life! A new being! Pulsating and growing within.

This is what Nanak means when he says:

'SABHANA JIYA KA EK DATA SO MAIN BISUR NA JAIE'!

The process begins from the gross and then it moves slowly and slowly to the subtle. Begin the remembrance consciously! Be aware! As the breath comes in flows the awareness of the message! And with the outgoing breath the awareness fills the outer environment! Together this process creates grooves in your consciousness.

'SABHANA JIYA KA EK DATA SO MAIN BISUR NA JAIE'!

The 'Jap' becomes 'Ajapa'. You move from the dimension of doing to non-doing! From action to no-action! From mind to no-mind!

Only then transcendence can really be possible.

'SABHANA JIYA KA EK DATA SO MAIN BISUR NA JAIE'!

Overflows an ecstatic Nanak!

VAHI GURU JI KA KHALSA VAHI GURU JI KE FATEH

Human body is composed of five elements: earth, fire, water, air and ether. These are matter. Matter decomposes. In the process tremendous energy is released. Body will surely perish one day.

Seek therefore that which is beyond matter. That which remains imprisoned within the four walls of the matter.

Know that as Allah or the LIGHT DIVINE. Seek eternal!